A Practical Guide to Canadian Political Economy

Wallace Clement
& Daniel Drache

James Lorimer & Company, Publishers

Toronto, 1978

ISBN 0-88862-184-1 cloth
0-88862-185-X paper

Cover design: Don Fernley

Canadian Cataloguing in Publication Data

Clement, Wallace.
A practical guide to Canadian political economy

ISBN 0-88862-184-1 bd. ISBN 0-88862-185-X pa.

1. Canada - Economic conditions - Bibliography.
I. Drache, Daniel, 1941- II. Title.

27165.C2C54 016.3309.71 C78-001170-8

James Lorimer & Company, Publishers
Egerton Ryerson Memorial Building
35 Britain Street
Toronto, Ontario

Printed and bound in Canada

CONTENTS

Acknowledgements

Special thanks to Barbara Stewart who checked the bibliography and to Lorraine Garry who graciously gave of her free time to act as library consultant. Thanks also to the editorial staff at James Lorimer and Company for their assistance and patience.

Preface

A political economy section of the Canadian Political Science Association was first organized at the 1976 Learned Societies Conference in Quebec City. These sessions marked the rebirth of Canadian political economy. In the field of publishing, the event has been welcomed by the publication of three collections: Close the 49th Parallel Etc., edited by Ian Lumsden; Capitalism and the National Question in Canada, edited by Gary Teeple; and most recently, The Canadian State: Political Economy and Political Power, edited by Leo Panitch. Each was sponsored by a loosely organized group of people known as SPEC (Studies in the Political Economy of Canada). This group is sponsoring the publication of the present bibliography and, as with its other publications, the royalties will return to the organization and be used to further additional critical studies of Canada's political economy.

This bibliography is a revised version of the one we distributed in September 1977 to subscribers to the Political Economy Network Newsletter, edited by Daniel Drache. It is being distributed in its current form by James Lorimer and Company to ensure its availability to a wider audience. It is hoped that those interested in the study of Canadian political economy will benefit from its contents and be assisted in both their teaching and independent research.

The readers of this bibliography will soon discover that the developments of the past few years have indeed been a "revival,", as Daniel Drache's introductory essay "Rediscovering Canadian Political Economy" makes clear. Canada has a long and important history in the political economy tradition, as is evident in the 1500 items included in the bibliography. The tradition has for some time now been neglected and researchers have tended to become prisoners of their disciplinary boundaries as the practitioners of economics, history, political science, social geography, anthropology, literature and sociology have created artificial boundaries around "their" areas to the relative neglect of the important roots each has in political economy. All have suffered from this narrowness and isolation.

For many years the social sciences in Canada have been dominated by perspectives and concerns emanating from the United Kingdom and the United States. The point has now been reached, however, where there exists in Canada a critical number of researchers and teachers able to sustain a distinctly Canadian perspective. The perspective which has been emerging is not a parochial one; it has drawn on theories developed elsewhere, particularly in Europe and Third World societies. But these theories are being expressly adopted to Canada's situation and applied critically to Canadian problems. Internationally, there has been an attempt to place Canada within the world system; internally, there has been an attempt to understand the effects of external relations on national developments.

At one time Canadian universities relied primarily on an outside labour pool for their teachers; now they are supplied from Canadian graduates. It is no longer necessary for most graduate students to go elsewhere to obtain a first-class education. The result is the building-up of a base of people within the Canadian academic community interested in Canadian society. The struggle is far from over. Canadian academics are only now beginning to rediscover their intellectual roots and indeed rediscover Canada as a subject of analysis. This is now a crucial period for stimulating and sustaining such a movement.

Much of the revival is the result of a renewed interest in radical scholarship with its roots in a broadly defined Marxist tradition, although political economy is by no means the sole domain of Marxists. The revival of both Marxism and political economy marks an invigoration of social science in Canada, an invigoration which combines an awareness of contemporary issues in Canadian society and a desire to do something about the Canadian condition. It has not, however, lost sight of the importance of history to the understanding of social change: indeed, some historians have been at the forefront in the revival. Furthermore, not all those influencing the revival are of a Marxist orientation. A good example is Carl Berger's The Writing of Canadian History, winner of the Governor General's award in 1976. This book provides an important, although biased, introduction to the key historical figures in Canadian political economy.

We have not attempted to provide a research document. It is rather a selective reading list, organized into meaningful categories, of available material, either published or forthcoming shortly, which the compilers feel merit attention. These readings can serve as an introduction to the student of political economy and as an impetus to researchers. A few research documents are now available, such as Primary Sources in Canadian Working Class History 1860-1930, edited by Hann, Kealey, Kealey and Warrian (Dumont Press, Kitchener, 1973) or, in a different vein, Manuel Gordon's Researching Canadian Corporations (New Hogtown Press, Toronto, 1977). These are important sources but serve a different purpose than the present Practical Guide, which attempts to acquaint readers with a broad range of literature on key topics which are all too often neglected in Canadian political economy. This document should stimulate Canadian studies and assist in developing the quality of Canadian social science.

There is no single overriding issue in Canadian political economy, but there are a series of features of the society which have emerged within the political economy tradition. These features help define questions appropriate to an analysis of Canada. At present they exist at the level of "pre-theory"; that is, observations and relationships deemed important but not yet integrated into a systematic explanatory framework. They are offered here as suggestions for further research:*

1. The implications of external relations for internal development, especially early colonial ties with France and the United Kingdom and the current dependence on the United States in many economic, political and military activities.

2. The origin of Canadian capitalism in a staple economy, its movement into commercial and financial specialization and its continued reliance on resource extraction.

3. The dependence on external markets, both as outlets for raw materials (making Canada vulnerable to world conditions) and as capital sources (which ultimately act as a drain on investment capital).

4. The effect of technology and the ownership of that technology, especially patent rights, in shaping the economy and labour force.

5. The go-between role Canada has in the world system, acting as an intermediary for many U.S.-based multinational corporations operating out of Canada and as a base for Canada's own multinationals, especially in finance.

---

*The following points are drawn from Wallace Clement, "Macrosociological Approaches Toward a 'Canadian Sociology'," Alternate Routes, 1, 1977.

6. The constraints imposed by geography, especially the rapids of the St. Lawrence, the Laurentian Shield, the Rockies and now, the North.

7. The tremendous costs of transportation networks from early roads, canals, ports, seaways and railways to pipelines for oil and gas, and their role in creating a national and continental economy.

8. The cultural dominance of English-speaking Canada by the United States through the arts, education and media, and the reactions to this through variants of nationalism.

9. The continued survival of two nations within a single state — the conquered French and the conquering English — and the demise of the native people, along with the reactions of these repressed minorities.

10. The continued active role of the Canadian state in the economy and its fragmented federal-provincial structure, aggravated by resource dependence and foreign investment.

11. The persistence of enormous regional differences within the country, especially the underdevelopment of the Atlantic region and the northern sections of the central and western provinces, as expressions of uneven development.

12. The role of immigration in filling the West during the early stages of development (1879 to 1914) and the urban centres of today (especially Montreal, Toronto and Vancouver) and in building an indigenous labour force and domestic market creating an ethnically diverse society stratified by class.

13. The persistence of a petty bourgeoisie class (largely farmers) as the most powerful class outside the capitalist class until World War II, prior to which Canada was largely rural and agrarian/resource based.

14. The continued existence of a large resource proletariat situated in isolated single-industry communities

built around mining, minerals, timber, pulp and paper, fishing and hydro-electric power.

15. The slower development of an urban industrial working class, the product of large-scale industrialization which did not become a dominant force in Canada until well into the twentieth century and which continues today to be rivalled in importance by the service sector of the labour force, especially the growing number of state workers adding to an already overdeveloped commercial sector.

Obviously these factors are related to each other. While various theories have been offered in the political economy tradition which order many of these components and purport to explain their relationships, none has been sufficiently developed to explain all of the features of Canada's political economy. This is a task which remains to be done. It is not one that a single individual can accomplish; it must be a collective task involving a great deal of original research and theorizing. It is in aid of this undertaking that we offer this bibliography, which we intend to revise in the future, and we welcome suggestions and additional entries from those who use this guide.

In compiling the bibliography, we would like to acknowledge the assistance of Carl Cuneo, David Frank, Craig Heron, Gerry Hunnius, Greg Kealey, Ralph Matthews, Tom Naylor, Leo Panitch, Norman Penner, Larry Pratt, Philip Resnick, Marylee Stephenson and Pauline Vaillancourt, who have all worked on specialized areas. For his usual thoroughness, Mel Watkins deserves special mention. We would also like to thank Studies in the Political Economy of Canada (SPEC) and Atkinson College, York University for providing funding and Elsie Clement for typing this material many times.

W.C. & D.D.

August 1978

REDISCOVERING CANADIAN POLITICAL ECONOMY

Daniel Drache

The Canadian political economy tradition is rich in insight and theoretical innovation. As one looks back on its unique and distinctive development, one is struck by the provocative and fruitful inquiry Canadian social scientists were engaged in. Indeed, Canadian social science reached levels of sophistication in the 1940s and early 1950s that have yet to be equalled.

This paper undertakes a survey of this tradition.* But a word of caution is in order at the outset: I have purposely sketched a very complex development in oversimplified terms. It seems to me to be particularly necessary at this point to see the general lines of development in an area of Canadian scholarship that for too long has suffered from neglect and, indeed, often deliberate disregard.

In this endeavour we find two theories of capitalist development based on the staple theory;[1] two approaches to the statist tradition of Canadian liberalism;[2] a welter of technical evidence on the performance and behaviour of the Canadian economy, with a great deal of valuable work done on capital formation;[3] a post-Innisian legacy which extended the economic dimension of the staple theory to include political, cultural, and constitutional questions;[4] an early Marxist grouping with special emphasis on Quebec and the corporate structure of Canadian capitalism;[5] and the challenging work of Fowke and other "hinterland" political economists in exposing internal metropolitan-hinterland relations.[6] Turning finally to more recent developments we find a spate of work examining the origins of Canadian capitalism, the nature of the Canadian bourgeoisie and Canada's crisis of development.[7]

*This paper is a revised version of an article which appeared in _Journal of Canadian Studies_, 9, no. 3 (August) 1976.

To do justice to this tradition in all its diversity, it is necessary to have a sense of its major parts. In its development it went through a number of phases and contains within it a number of distinct directions of inquiry. If we include what could be termed the "interregnum" as well as the most recent group of Marxist political economists, we may distinguish seven fairly well-defined phases. While any typology of this kind is open to criticism, the following break-down will provide a convenient and I hope fruitful way of approaching the question.

The Founders: amongst whom are counted Innis, Creighton, Mackintosh, Lower and Morton. It is in this group that we find the theoretical foundation of the tradition, focusing on Canada's locus and role in the world economy. At the same time we find in this group two strikingly different and, indeed, opposed views of Canadian industrialisation and development.

The "State Theorists": including Underhill, Corry, Hodgetts, Scott, Forsey and Trudeau. This group had as its central and key focus the interventionist and social role of the Canadian state.

The "University of Toronto Practitioners": In the development of Canadian political economy these political economists - Easterbrook, Dales, Bladen, Clarke, Aitken, *et al.* - were responsible for the revision of Innis.

The "Hinterlanders": those who focused on the internal pattern of dependency and uneven development, e.g. Fowke, Britnell, Buckley, Soward and Saunders.

The "Post-Innisians": including Mallory, Macpherson, McLuhan, Pentland, Spelt, Ferns and Aitken, in whose writings we find an elaboration of the Innis model in terms of superstructural relations.

The "Launderers": Deutsch, Porter, Careless, Brecher, Reisman and many others who trivialized political economy by discarding the economic basis of the discipline.

The New Political Economy: including the writings of Ryerson, Nelles, Watkins, Naylor and Clement, among others, who from a Marxist or neo-Marxist perspective have revived the political economy tradition.

As is obvious, not everyone fits into these groups. There is much overlap and movement in and out over time, and some political economists fall between categories. Caves and Holton,[8] for instance, straddle the "Post-Innisians" and the "Launderers"; Creighton's work has shifted markedly over his long career while Easterbrook[9] has contributed studies in political economy belonging to several of our groupings. The categories are meant to be suggestive of the trends, issues, and emphases developed over a fifty-year period.

Innis and Mackintosh are singled out as pivotal. They represent the two major streams in the Canadian school of political economy, the differences between which are crucial to its development. While they began in the same tradition, they came to hold radically different global perspectives on Canada and on political economy. The Mackintosh view could perhaps be summed up in the title of Lower's work Colony to Nation: Canadian political economy was a trajectory leading towards a viable autonomous nation in the universal framework of the international market economy. Innis held the opposite view ("No country has more to fear from the new internationalism than Canada"), and Canadian history was on the point of being reversed: "Canada [had] moved from colony to nation to colony."[10] On the key question of the staple, their respective theories of economic growth and capitalist development were diametrically opposed. From 1920 to the mid-1950s their approaches to the study of political economy crystallized around very different conceptions of what was happening to Canada socially, economically and politically, and these conceptions were reflected throughout their writing and research.

In speaking of schools of thought in Canadian political economy, one must consider general theoretical frameworks, common assumptions, converging lines of analysis and agreement on basic issues.[11] In these respects Mackintosh's position was the more systematic, with a coherent view of the state, economic development and the nature of industrial society, all built around a basic theory of incremental growth.[12] Innis' legacy, by comparison, is more diffuse and is animated by a more critical sense of inquiry. Its focus on the nature of Canada's continued dependence status makes it, in the end, a far more powerful basis for an analysis of Canadian society.

Although for a long period there was no resolution of the tension and conflict between the Innis and Mackintosh approaches, one school did of course become dominant. In the mid-fifties, the Innis model of centre-margin relations was abandoned. It is this series of events which provides the key to the fate of Canadian political economy.

A Snapshot of the Canadian School

What is the political economy tradition and what are some of its accomplishments? In its largest sense political economy, including the Canadian variant, is the study of the laws and relations of capitalist development, either critically from the Marxist perspective or more traditionally from the liberal view which affirms the legitimacy of the capitalist social system.[13] It is often forgotten that Marxist and liberal political economists share certain common assumptions. Both believe that the task of political economy is to identify and analyze social relations as they relate to the economic system of production. Both have (though from radically different standpoints) a world view of the present epoch which is conscious of bourgeois relations.[14] Both insist that the mode of production is the organic link which orders the social relations between the economy and society. Finally, political economy is a study of society as an integrated whole, based on contributions from social scientists from all disciplines.[15]

The Canadian tradition developed mainly within the broad framework of liberal political economy and took seriously the task of producing a social theory of Canada which would begin to explain capitalist relations. Even today, a generation later, the staples theory and the Laurentian school remain, despite their inadequacies, the most viable interpretations of Canadian history. They demonstrate better than anything else how political economy attempts to understand social relations in terms of the mode of production. For both Innis and Creighton the political economy of Canada evolved out of the control exercised by the imperial presence of an external economy.

Furthermore, the Canadian school stressed the need to study Canada by means of a perspective based in Canada. The extent to which the Canadian school altered the Smith-Mill tradition to fit its own needs is revealing. The focus was shifted away from an inquiry "into the nature and wealth of nations" towards an examination of the incompleteness of national development, with the stress on the social rigidities produced by uneven growth. The students of Canadian political economy rejected the idea that American scholarship in this area was applicable to the Canadian case. In their view Canada and the United States were two recognizably distinct social systems, each requiring a distinct approach. In their study of imperial policy, colonial economy and class as a social force, there is a very different basic focus and a critical stance. Initially, at least, the perspective was not technocratic or hegemonic, though it tended to move in those directions.

At the same time, it is important to recognize that much is missing from the Canadian tradition as it evolved. For instance, the work on external dependence remained incomplete, even though there is a wealth of literature on internal dependence between Eastern interests and the revolt of the West.[16] Similarly, there have been few studies on the working class or the distribution of wealth among classes,[17] which is surprising in view of the fact that this had been an area of considerable interest in nineteenth as well as early twentieth-century liberal political economy in England, as in the case of J.A. Hobson, one of the last great English contributors to the tradition. Again, there is little work done on Quebec and its political struggles within Confederation, Ryerson of course being the exception. (Innis and Creighton were, however, sensitive to a certain degree to the destruction of the native peoples.)[18] Finally, although there was consciousness of imperialism both as a historical problem and as an analytical concept, most of the school failed to see the United States in this light and no one developed a theory of imperialism in terms of a class analysis, or anything remotely approaching an examination of the social origins of imperialism.[19] Counterbalancing these shortcomings is the tremendous energy that went into the examination, often in great depth, of social relations, institutions, and the economic system of Canada.[20]

These accomplishments, involving relatively few people, raise some serious questions about Canadian social science in general and political economy in particular. Why was it possible for a distinctive Canadian social science to emerge while Canada was still a British dependency? Why was this tradition abandoned? Conversely, why has political economy re-emerged after a long sleep and once again become a focus for many young academics?

There have been some attempts to address these questions in recent years, though the answers fail to be very convincing. How does one explain the fact that V.W. Bladen, in a work just published on the political economy tradition,[21] begins with Adam Smith and ends with Keynes while totally ignoring the Canadian tradition? This is the more remarkable in that this tradition was a notable product of the British school. I cannot see this omission as simply a case of neglect. It falls into the category of cultural amnesia: the loss of historical memory which is a much deeper and more serious problem.

Another observation strikes me as very puzzling. In surveying recent Canadian political science, one is struck by the number of eminent writers who, after having made one major contribution (Mallory and Macpherson, for instance), have failed to extend their research into other areas of Canadian political economy.[22] The inability or unwillingness to theorize on Canadian relations is itself a matter of profound importance. When it occurs, as it has, on a large scale, it becomes a social problem in its own right. It produces an intellectual and cultural void. Scientific inquiry without a capacity for synthetic and original thinking is an exercise in social autism. This failure is an acute symptom of a larger problem.[23]

Another illustration of this phenomenon is the disappearance of political economy from Canadian universities in the context of growing cultural domination by the United States during the fifties. It should be recalled that the euphemism used at the time to discredit political economy was the necessity to "modernize" Canadian social science. Behind this attitude was the belief that political economy was parochial and backward, somehow out of date with current developments, particularly those in the United States.[24] Since most people in the universities at the time complied with this judgement, Canada's academics must accept responsibility for their part in burying the political economy tradition. An unpublished survey done in 1973 of sixty-five political science departments[25] showed that in the case of at least ninety per cent no provision was being made for the study of Canadian political economy. Some retained the name of the discipline in the title of the department, but there was little evidence that this made any difference to their curricula. Only a few universities made any attempt to maintain a Canadian school of political economy. The conclusion is inescapable. American social science had overwhelmed what was a uniquely Canadian tradition of scholarship, so that today political economy has only a marginal existence in Canadian universities.

It is particularly unsettling to realize that the university community accepted the loss of this discipline with equanimity. On the whole, opposition was minimal, though there were, of course, a few exceptions. Hilda Neatby's attack on the new educational philosophy as part of an American cultural vanguard is one instance of resistance.[26] George Grant's polemic against Canada's ruling circles is another, more recent dissenting voice.[27] Somewhat belatedly, James Eayrs, in his Plaunt Lectures, was one of the few academics who had a public change of heart about the cold war cultural shock waves emanating from New York, Boston, and Chicago.[28] He spoke of "shifting out of neutral" and of the need for a reassessment of the era of cold war social science. Significantly, none of these objections crystallized into a centre of opposition or started an alternative school rooted in earlier Canadian thought.

The answer to the question of why political economy was abandoned needs to be pursued along quite different lines, different even from the ones put forth by Cairns and Smiley.[29] Their attempts have been suggestive but have stopped short of confronting the larger issue. The break with political economy was a break with materialism. It is this crucial aspect of the problem that has been generally overlooked. As a result it has been difficult to understand what was being rejected and why. Not surprisingly, therefore, discussions about political economy remain amorphous and ill-defined, shrouded in nostalgia and ignorance.

Let us turn now to a brief overview of the development of the Canadian tradition in an attempt to discover why it suffered the fate it did.

The Development and Disintegration of Canadian Political Economy

The Founders

As was suggested above, the founders of the political economy tradition in Canada did the pioneering work on the staple, and it was through this inquiry that they were able to present a coherent analysis of the internal and external forces that have come to shape Canada.[30] The staple theory traces the influence of trade, development, settlement and imperial policy on national development. Creighton used the staple framework to write his great history of the empire of the St. Lawrence. The economic relations of commercial imperialism provide the basic perspective of his social and political history of imperial policy in the British North American colonies.[31] Innis provided the larger view of the staple in studying the central place of the export of resources to more advanced economies under the French regime, British mercantilism, middle British imperialism and finally American monopoly capitalism. Mackintosh in turn developed the staple as a theory of economic growth, stressing the connection between the external demand for Canadian resources and the attainment of a mature industrial society. W.L. Morton further explored the centralizing tendencies of a staple-dominated development in terms of an internal metropolitan relationship between Central Canada and the exploitation of the West.[32]

The studies of the "Founders" constitute a primary body of knowledge and research on the development of Canadian capitalism from its pre-industrial origins to the end of the National Policy. But the most important aspect of the Founders' writing is their theory of capitalist development, with its stress on the staple. In this regard Innis and Mackintosh figure prominently.

The central idea of Innis' theory is that for Canada, unlike European countries, the motor of development is not manufacturing but the growth of export-led sectors: furs, fish, timber, wheat, industrial minerals and energy products. His theory explained economic development — particularly the stages of that development — in terms of the primary economic relations and how in Canada these involve the demand for and the export of raw materials to a foreign imperialist centre.

Innis thus developed a theory of centre-margin relations under capitalism. When he spoke of the import-export of resources he was as much interested in the set of social relations that are being imported and exported as in the actual trade picture *per se*.[33] While the two are inseparable it is the former relation pertaining to the mode of development which he termed the staple approach and which forms the important part of Innis' theory. This is how he elaborates the way in which the staple concretizes those relations:

> Concentration on the production of staples for export to more highly industrialized areas in Europe and later in the U.S. had broad implications for the Canadian economic, political and social structure. Each staple in its turn left its stamp, and the shift to a new staple invariably produced periods of crises in which adjustments in the old structure were painfully made and a new pattern created in relation to a new staple.[34]

Once expanded, the staple theory entails the following:

- the economy in a dependency is tied to the economy in a foreign industrial centre by market and trade relations;
- the development of productive forces at the margin will follow the developments in the imperial centre; in short, the imperial power selects those staples which it requires on terms favourable to itself;
- the staple economy is invariably subject to crises and disruption because it is neither self-generating nor self-regulating;
- the staple economy is distorted because of the demands of an external economy for resources and, conversely, remains underdeveloped with regard to industry. As Innis says: "The trade in staples characterizes an economically weak country";[35]
- the relations between the centre and margin are further distorted by unequal trade relations, heavy fixed overhead cost and the constant outflow of capital in the form of investment income to foreign

financial centres.

Innis came to the conclusion that in Canada industrialism would be a dependent process, since the export of staples primes the industrial pump of the imperialist economy, not Canada's. Canada, he believed, would continue to be a net exporter of resources and a net importer of manufactured goods relying on borrowed technology. It was inherent in the imperial-colonial relationship that Canada would be prevented from becoming a net producer of manufactured goods in the world economy.

By contrast, the Mackintosh theory of the staple was overly simple. He presented the trade in staples to an external economy as the only way forward for developing a pioneer society: "Nothing is more typical of colonial development than the restless, unceasing search for staples which would permit the pioneer community to come into close contact with the commercial world and leave behind the disabilities of a pioneer existence."[36] Mackintosh was in effect elaborating a stage theory of growth that stressed the creation of an internal market through settlement; the demand pull of the world economy as a market; the expansion of economic activity by the building of an infra-structure; and, finally, the establishment of industries to supply initially the home market and settler needs and later the world market for goods. The great challenge that faced every colonial country, Mackintosh believed, was to put into motion an economic programme that brought together the above factors.

In Canada, the key to economic takeoff was the opening of the West. But before its leading commodity could be exported and the West settled, a transportation system was needed. Transportation was the link that connected Canada to its overseas markets, facilitated settlement, stimulated the expansion of home industries and brought the economy into the industrial age. The intensification of economic activity depended upon the prosperity generated through the exploitation of Canada's resources by the world economy.

Mackintosh's model of development was, in large measure, borrowed from the American experience.[37] Canada was launched on a parallel course of development. The frontier, the building of a transcontinental railway system, the transformation of river valleys into industrial centres, the heavy borrowing abroad — all prominent features of American expansion — had their Canadian counterparts. To the extent that Canada would remain the poor man's version of the United States, Mackintosh attributed this to the harshness of the environment and the barrenness of the Shield. Mackintosh's optimism about the development of the Canadian economy stemmed from his assessment that through the process of incremental growth Canada had left its economic colonial heritage behind. In the early twenties he was confident that Canada had come of age. It would be only a matter of time before Canada's industrial revolution would be complete. He summarized his views with these self-confident words: "It behooves present day historians to perceive...the story of a people facing the prosaic obstacles of a colonial existence, developing national traits and winning through to nationhood."[38]

Their divergent theories of the staple led Innis and Mackintosh to radically different assessments of Canadian capitalist relations. Mackintosh was a passionate believer in capitalism as an essentially progressive system. Innis was a critic of capitalism who increasingly came to believe that it betrayed its own values. Mackintosh accepted the view that a colonial dependency was helped to maturity by an imperial country, whereas Innis countered that precisely because there was no break with the powerful metropolitan economy Canadian independence was at best a doubtful proposition. Mackintosh argued that the export-led growth and expansion was the basis of industrial development: the era of the colonial staple prepared a settler country for gradual and eventual industrialization. Innis, conversely, held the view that Canada's staple-oriented economy would remain fundamentally dependent because centre-margin relations under capitalism are such that dependencies are prevented from developing into self-generating industrialized economies.

The work of Innis and Mackintosh provided the basic framework for the subsequent study of Canadian development. Innis' writing laid the foundation for a critical tradition of political economy; Mackintosh's dominated the hegemonic tradition, legitimizing capitalist relations. For the next thirty-five years their respective views of nationality and imperialism, the nature of Canadian industrialization, the strength of a staple economy, Canada's relations with the United States and the role of Canada in the world economy sustained both traditions.

The "State Theorists": Liberal Reformers and Social Democrats

The work of this group covers the two distinct eras of the Rowell-Sirois Report and the post-war reconstruction phase. Leaving aside the erratic and, in the end, disappointing development of Underhill's writing,[39] the political economy we find here is held together by a common perspective on the role of the Canadian state and Canadian federalism. Their research and theorizing have had considerable political impact since they have influenced government thinking on these matters.

Corry did some of the most significant early research on the interventionist nature of the Canadian state. In his pioneering but now neglected study of the state done for the Rowell-Sirois Commission,[40] he discovered that from the time of Confederation the Canadian state has acted as a social regulator in a wide range of areas in public and private life and particularly as regards economic development, where the state has frequently been the principal funding agency of the private sector. Corry identifies the peculiar bent of Canadian liberalism: in Canada the State is assigned an active role differing from the non-interventionist philosophy of more industrialized societies. In showing the absence of a laissez-faire tradition, Corry was laying the legal and theoretical groundwork for justifying a powerful federal authority.

We find another important aspect to the statist tradition in Corry's research. While he was not particularly interested in developing a class analysis of Canadian society (in the manner of, say, C.B. Macpherson), Corry's work is germane in showing that the Canadian state, originally fashioned as an instrument of British policy, retained much of its colonial character after Confederation. The statist tradition of Canadian liberalism is thus found to be firmly rooted in the particularities of Canadian economic and political dependence. The Canadian state began as a powerful entity because there was no other agency capable of directing life in our form of pioneer society. The State was relied upon extensively to carry out the programme and many of the functions more normally thought of as the responsibilities of a national bourgeoisie. In some respects at least the state became a substitute for that class. Hodgetts' later work on the pioneer public service is a further elaboration and expansion of the inquiry into the early origins of the Canadian state.[41]

Scott and Forsey (and later, Trudeau) have played an equally important role in this area of Canadian political economy by above all helping to develop the social framework for the Liberal government immediately following the Second World War. Their work on the public sector is, however, also important because of their influence in moving the focus of political economy away from a dependency model. They elaborated, with the help of British and American counterparts, a technocratic model of social relationships.

Scott's writing on legal and constitutional questions laid an important foundation for increasing the government's role in a wide range of social services.[42] In assigning the state a social purpose formerly lacking, the social democrats were elaborating the fundamental tenet of their philosophy, that Parliament and the rule of law could be made the instrument of all classes and not simply that of the ruling elites. Their belief was that education, research and the introduction of modern technology lead to better government, more planning and a set of administrators more in tune with the needs of the people. The technocratic vision downgraded the politics of the workplace, the ideology of class struggle and concern for Canada's national integrity. In this fashion the social democratic theorists changed the scope of inquiry of Canadian political economy by severing the connection between property relations and the social basis of the state. In their treatment of the state they did not simply overstress the importance of the social sphere at the expense of the material forces of production; they removed the state from its historical, national and class setting.

The "University of Toronto Practitioners"

This group is significant mainly because it blocked the development of the Innis tradition. Innis was preoccupied with the themes of nationality and imperialism.[43] His concept of political economy laid particular emphasis on the fact that Canada's colonial journey was not over and that the continuing weakness of the Canadian state was due in large measure to the trade in resources controlled by the United States. The study of political economy played an important role in articulating the issue of imperialism and its implications for Canada. The "University of Toronto Practitioners" rejected categorically that part of Innis' theory which opposed the policies and the influence of the new American imperialism. Although often identifying itself with the work of Innis, the Department of Political Economy at the University of Toronto has done little to advance the tradition he initiated. It is paradoxical that the university where Innis did his pioneering work became a stronghold of American approaches to economic study and one of the most vigorous centres of the philosophy of continentalism - the economic strategy of dependence.

This university department was influential in obscuring the Innis legacy in another important respect. By concentrating on only one aspect of Innis' work and viewing his writing on economic history in a rather narrow specialist's sense, they ignored the broader vision and insight that Innis brought to the study of the history of the staple. Aitken's work is an eloquent and isolated exception: it is the most substantial and impressive study of American capital and Canadian resources done in the sixties — significantly, it was published in the United States rather than in Canada.[44]

The "Hinterlanders"

In this grouping I have termed the "Hinterlanders," we find political economists who studied and analyzed the features of internal dependency, primarily between the West and Central Canada. Many of them taught in Canada's Western universities.[45] They concentrated their attention on the policies of national development as seen from a hinterland perspective. The work of Fowke and Buckley on the National Policy, the wheat economy and capital formation are particularly impressive contributions analyzing the internal chain of exploitation and the price system as it affected regional development and the class position of the independent commodity producers of Western Canada.[46]

Fowke's account of the state aspect of the National Policy showing its links with the railways, banks and industrial monopolies challenged the orthodox nationalist interpretation of its aims. With admirable care for meticulous detail, he showed how the National Policy drained the economic surplus out of the producers' hands and into the hands of the appropriating class, setting the stage for the farmers' epic struggle against Eastern capitalism. Farmers have often been seen as the motor of Canadian development in the first three decades of this century. Fowke's analysis of the rrots of this conflict is the most impressive documentation of uneven development at the regional level. He concentrated his attention primarily on the internal aspects of the chain of exploitation. Although not unaware of external linkages, Fowke believed that the main problem was the internal rather than external structure.

The work of the Hinterlanders is impressive in showing the economic basis of regional disparity from a class point of view, but at the same time this perspective reveals some surprising gaps. They did not link the phenomenon of regionalism to the external force of imperialism, inasmuch as the economic surplus was not destined solely for Eastern banks. Similarly, they paid little attention to resource exploitation in other sectors. The Western Hinterlanders tended to overlook the existence of a resource-based proletariat with the potential of being powerful allies of the prairie farm movements. The hinterland perspective runs into further difficulty by analyzing internal dependency strictly from the standpoint of the individual commodity producers. Wheat was a resource like coal, wood products, base metals and energy. To a very important degree the social relations of all the resource sectors were heavily influenced, if not controlled, by an outside economy. The Hinterlanders never came to terms with the problem of external dependence and in large measure this reflects the populist influence on their model of political economy. The bigness of industry is stressed, rather than its ownership and control. Because they never got a grip on these broader issues, the hinterland model leaves important questions unresolved. Even though Fowke's analysis showed that the farmers were unsuccessful in influencing Ottawa to curb the power of the banks and the railways as well as to reform the terms of the National Policy, he failed to develop a theory of the Canadian state as a capitalist institution. This prevented him from providing a comprehensive answer to what hindered the state from protecting the legitimate aspirations of the Western farmers.

That these issues come to the fore reflects the analytical power of the hinterland perspective. In many ways the work done on Canada's hinterland has been the most productive, detailed and perceptive contribution of the Canadian school of political economy.

The Post-Innisians

As the name suggests, what characterizes these contributions to Canadian political economy is their attempt to carry on the Innis tradition of studying the social relations of a staple-dominated model of production. They refine the Innis viewpoint by extending his basic approach to include superstructural relations, as in Mallory's and Macpherson's studies of the constitution and political parties respectively.[47] McLuhan's examination of industrial culture is a contribution to cultural anthropology of a more general nature, dealing with the character of culture under capitalism.[48] Ferns[49] and Pentland[50] undertook the first substantial Canadian investigation of the working class and the development of the modern industrial relations system. Spelt's too often overlooked examination of industrialization in South-central Ontario complements Innis' work on the staple economy and fills in a much neglected aspect of the transition from a resource economy to a regionally industrialized economy in Central Canada.[51] What the industrial pattern reveals is that industrialism was forced to accommodate itself to Canada's hinterland status and to create its own hinterland in turn. South-central Ontario is a classic illustration of the metropolitan-hinterland thesis. By using its strategic position it was able to control trade and commerce nationally, as well as influence the industrial pattern throughout the rest of the country through Toronto-based banks and manufacturing concerns.

The above studies constitute an extremely important body of knowledge about Canada with regard to: 1) a class analysis of political parties; 2) the influence of capitalist relations on the changing character of Canadian federalism; 3) a theory of commodity culture; 4) the class nature of the industrial relations system; and 5) the beginning of a regional theory of capitalist development.

It is noteworthy that the studies of the three M's (Mallory, Macpherson and McLuhan) contain what might be called a critical stance toward the question of the social relations of capitalism. They were not anti-capitalist in the way Miliband is in The State and Capitalist Society or the way Ryerson is in writing on Quebec and Canada.[52] Nor were they "neutral" in the sense, increasingly implied in this term, of failing to recognize class interests or class relationships as primary social forces. They occupied a more genuinely middle ground, being interested in the institutional expression of class relations without necessarily advocating an alternative to capitalism *per se*. This is how Macpherson explained the partial terms of his inquiry into the party system: "The party system characteristically performs a function that is indispensable for democracy within a mature capitalist society: it moderates and contains the opposition of class interest."[53] Much of the same tone of critical detachment is found in McLuhan's and Mallory's writings. Even Ferns' examination of the bitterly fought evolution of Canadian industrial relations shared much the same tone.[54] These were not angry works; nonetheless, they are effective in penetrating the facade of social relationships. One of their notable accomplishments is to demonstrate a radically different approach to the study of institutions and a sharp break with the constitutional/institutional studies of Dawson (The Government of Canada) and others. That their efforts have lasting merit is due in no small measure to their success in explaining the social development of Canadian institutions as a response to the changing class structure and economy of Canada.

Mallory's use of the Innis legacy is in some ways the most unique application. Social Credit and the Federal Power of Disallowance is seminal in a number of respects since it focuses on an explanation of the economic basis of Canadian federalism. Mallory identifies the latter as the power to control capital formation and protect property relations, and in so doing presents us with an entirely novel view of federal-provincial relations and the constitutional decisions of the Privy Council. The tangled history of Canadian jurisprudence relates to Canada's quasi-colonial status, to use Macpherson's term. Mallory shows how the Privy Council interpretations of key clauses in Canada's constitution were more appropriate to British custom than to Canadian needs and reality.[55] On the key issue of the role of the state in the economy, British jurisprudence applied an essentially laissez-faire doctrine which when applied to Canada, hamstrung federal initiative in a wide range of policy matters.

In addition to this, Mallory takes up the broader issue involved in Social Credit's head-on collision with Ottawa and finance capital. He forces us to go outside the traditional categories of interpreting judicial review by showing the linkages between the evolution of that tradition and the needs of capitalist relations. He examines why Canada's constitution is the embodiment of a staple economy controlled externally for such a large part of its history, and how from the outset it was biased in terms of the powers it conferred on a central authority to conduct trade in staples. By means of this framework Mallory is able to explain brilliantly that the drift towards a centralized federalism is a function of the centralizing tendencies within capital itself. In the final analysis, Mallory is demonstrating the phenomenon that judicial interpretation, the structure of the constitution, the division of powers, etc. make sense only in relation to Canada's quasi-colonial status and the class interests of Canadian capitalists.

McLuhan uses a similar starting point for an examination of mass culture.[56] Culture in industrial society is an expression of the relations of commodity production, particularly commodity fetishism. In the era of monopoly capitalism, or mature capitalism, culture is no longer primarily the expression of tradition, folkways, the family, history, religion, etc. Just as capitalism destroys the earlier mode of production, it also uproots and recreates culture in its own image. McLuhan takes this central idea as his starting point and studies modern advertising as the source of the new dominant expression of culture.

Again, this is an extension of Innis' work on technology and communications, though in a way that shows the originality of McLuhan as a social theorist (a quality that is, however, noticeably missing from most of his more recent writing). Though McLuhan's work is not specifically on Canada, the development of an Americanized mass culture and its export to the English-speaking world raises important questions of Canada's ability to survive the American cultural onslaught. In <u>Counterblast</u>, his surrealist cultural manifesto published in 1954, McLuhan remonstrates against the American cultural invasion of Canada. He does this in a way that avoids a simple-minded anti-Americanism, reflecting rather the sentiments of a much broader anti-imperialist cultural critique. In his manifesto he links the lack of Canadian resistance to the commodity "blitz-krieg" to the policies of the domestic colonial elite. Here is a brief sampling of his imaginative cultural polemic:

Oh B L A S T

The MASSEY REPORT damp cultural igloo
for canadian devotees of
T I M E
&
L I F E

Oh B L A S T nursery politics and
Henry Goose on the Loose. The cring-
ing, flunkey spirit of canadian culture, its
servant-quarter snobbishness
resentments
ignorance
penury
OTTAWA tomb of talent
fount of dullness
snorkel centre of underwater
thought and orders-in-council...
B L E S S
The MASSEY REPORT,
HUGE RED HERRING for
derailing Canadian kulcha while it is
absorbed by American ART & Technology.

MASSEY-HARRIS farm machinery, Canada's
  REAL contribution to CULTURE
BLESS
    Our Sense of Our Density
The Canadian JACKPINE, hardy citizen
 of the WORLD'S MOST ANCIENT ROCK.

The Laurentian Shield, TROJAN HORSE
bringing American capital to Canada....

McLuhan broaches the question of imperialism in the cultural domain and sets the stage for a larger work on the subject which of course is never forthcoming. Nonetheless, both The Mechanical Bride and his cultural commentary remain pioneer contributions in bridging the gaps between culture, technology and the economy.

Even this brief sampling of the post-Innisians demonstrates the relatively sophisticated development of political economy in integrating economic and social theory. Pentland's analysis of the origins of the Canadian working class and Ferns' study of the institution of industrial relations also deserve mention in this respect.

It is interesting too that several of the post-Innisians use a basically Marxist framework of analysis. In this tradition, Macpherson's classic study, Democracy in Alberta: Social Credit and the Party System — one wishes it had been titled more appropriately to indicate its broader scope — remains one of the few works produced in the English language synthesizing traditional political theory with a class analysis of the political system. Although a highly original work and a classic in Canadian political economy, it nevertheless remains a curiously unfinished exploration of the Canadian party system. Macpherson's examination of Social Credit brings out only one aspect of Canadian dependence, viz. at the provincial and regional levels. He does not show us how his class analysis would apply to either the working class or the politics of the bourgeoisie. Nevertheless, the model is there for such an undertaking, even though it may require further elaboration and refinement.

However, Macpherson's study does show how the Canadian political system diverges sharply from both British and American traditions in maintaining a quasi-party system at the provincial level. But Macpherson only hints at the broader ramifications of this analysis at the level of national politics. He makes the fundamental observation that "we appear to be moving into a period in which the class function is becoming the more important function of the party system."[57] He goes on to note: "The conditions that gave rise to it in Alberta are not entirely lacking in Canada as a whole. As Canada becomes increasingly overshadowed by the more powerful economy of the United States, her position approximates the quasi-colonial."[58] Within this general framework Macpherson provides some possible clues as to the general dynamics of Canada's political system. He points out, for instance, that "a quasi-colonial society in which independent producers are the predominant element appears peculiarly liable to both kinds of quasi-party system."[59]

In a broader theoretical framework, what all this underscores is that Canada's quasi-colonial status produces a weak variant of the two-party system and, equally, that radical populism of the left or the right cannot offer any fundamental challenge. Although Macpherson does not explain the basis of a working-class politics, his perspective does bring into focus some of the essential elements of a theory of Canadian politics in the context of Canada's quasi-colonial status and the broad class divisions that continue to dominate it.

Re-reading Macpherson twenty years after his book was written, one is forced to reflect upon his early critique of pluralism and the degree to which his own work in democratic theory offered an alternative to American and British scholarship in the field. At that time he wrote, "Orthodox twentieth-century political science has in effect neutralized democratic theory, while still trying to uphold democratic values." He explains that this development has its antecedent in economics:

> There is an obvious parallel between the transformation of political economy into economics after Ricardo and that of political thought or philosophy — the term was never precise — into political science after John Stuart Mill. The change came a little later (and is not yet as advanced) in political science, but it is the same change; the humanistic substance is taken out, supposedly in the interests of more refined scientific handling of the problems.[60]

The events which Macpherson noted are particularly germane to our examination of the Canadian school of political economy. They deeply affected the general development of political economy in Canada. Those around Mackintosh came to believe that political economy had exhausted its usefulness in terms of the questions posed and the answers found. Political economy came to be regarded as lacking scientific precision and rigour. The new social science would be one which recognized Canada as being on an equal footing with the rest of the advanced capitalist world. Political economy hence was inappropriate to the study of a modern Canada. This was the turn of events which opened the door for accepting a "generalized" social science, mainly of American vintage. Thus, what was vital and unique to Canadian social science — the possibility of theorizing Canadian society critically and independently — was lost. The most significant period of Canadian scholarship ended after a renaissance of less than a decade!

The "Launderers"

The discipline of political economy was, however, not entirely abandoned in the fifties. As the term "laundering" is meant to suggest, it was cleaned up and made more palatable in the era of American social science. Only part of the tradition was retained, while many vital aspects were discarded. In the first instance, political economy was reduced to economic history in which the centre-margin theory and the stress on dependency were played down. The chronicling of the phases of growth, with the stress on detailed factual accounts, replaced the broad theoretical issue of capitalist development. Easterbrook and Aitken's Canadian Economic History was the most influential work published in this genre.

Political economy underwent further change in the hands of Buckley, Bertram, and Caves and Holton,[61] who attempted to quantify the staple model in one or another of its aspects. Under their influence political economy was reduced to providing data for econometric studies of the Canadian economy. They confined themselves to explaining the economy in its technical aspects — how it functioned and operated — and they abandoned altogether any attempt to link the system of capitalism to its social milieu.

The laundering of political economy was not confined to contributions from economists. Porter's Vertical Mosaic reveals much the same process at work. Published in the mid-sixties, it was a compendium of social statistics documenting the twin issues of inequality and elitism. The class analysis which had played such a prominent part in Macpherson's study of the party system had been dropped altogether. Porter's theoretical framework — to the extent that there was one — was drawn primarily from American and European sources. Even though the book focused on the corporate interlocks and the concentration of power among Canada's business class, there was minimal discussion of Canada as a social formation. Surprisingly, the Canadian economy and its external linkages received only passing attention. In reading Porter, one is hard pressed to know in what respect Canadian society is appreciably different from British and American, the models on which his study was uncritically based.

Much the same point could be raised with regard to the treatment of metropolitanism by historians. In "Frontierism and Metropolitanism,"[62] Careless reinterpreted the metropolitan thesis of Innis and Creighton and stripped it of its critical insights. He overemphasized rather crudely the environmentalism of Innis and Creighton and understated the implicit economic theory of capitalist development and capitalist relations. The question of imperialism barely received mention. The focus is turned almost exclusively in one direction: the rise of the modern metropole as a dominant centre of trade, commerce, communications and culture. Again, what emerges is a generalized view of modern capitalism. In this particular presentation, metropolitanism is difficult to distinguish from urbanology, the rise of the modern city.

What characterized the laundering of political economy was the tendency to let the national dimension drop out of sight and along with it any attempt to examine the social relations of Canadian capitalism. Macpherson makes the point that the fate of political economy was decided by developments occurring primarily in the discipline of economics. Both the Marshallian and the Keynesian revolutions had, of course, a profound impact on the study of economics, the effect of which was to push the older tradition of political economy aside.[63] But even allowing for this shift, Canadian social scientists have shown a remarkable lack of interest in the body of work on the economy which nevertheless has continued to come out of the political economy tradition. Most striking in this regard is the lack of attention Canadian dependency has received from Canada's academic community. Even though one can point to the Massey and particularly to the Gordon Royal Commission, as well as to the governmental agencies which provide source material for such inquiries, on the whole the issue has simply been ignored. Hence, until recently, Canada's pivotal relations with the United States remained largely a non-question in the body of Canadian social science. It was not taken seriously as an issue worthy of scholarly attention.

The insularity of this view, which does not value an understanding of the economy in its largest sense as a necessary and important object of social inquiry, has very broad implications. It leads to a fatal inability to take into account the organic connection between the economic system of capitalism and its social relations. Once this tie had been severed, Canadian history, economics, politics, literature, industrial relations, etc. could be studied as totally compartmentalized entities without regard for, or a sense of, any of the larger structures and issues that determine them.[64]

What replaced political economy in the fifties was a social science based upon reconstructed theories of elitism, managerialism, bureaucracy, the imperatives of technology, etc., all heavily infused with a particular class view of human nature. Problems were examined independently of one another and without reference to economic relations. The swing away from political economy was also encouraged from the United States, where academics, using the prestige and influence of their professional associations as well as covert government agencies, launched a cultural campaign against traditions of scholarship that diverged sharply from the American way. This applied not only to Marxism but also to liberal political economy within the United States and in other countries which stressed social determinism and the study of imperialism, or openly challenged the American "internationalist" stance. In such an atmosphere, Canadian intellectuals were unprepared to defend their own traditions. The Canadian political economy approach was, in effect, suppressed.

The treatment of Innis' place in Canadian letters is noteworthy in this connection. The Innis era came to be regarded as a keepsake, a memento from an era long past. His work was trivialized and its importance obscured. Canadian political economy ended up as exotica.

The further development of a distinctive Canadian perspective was replaced with the canons and models of American cold-war social science.

The New Political Economy

The new political economy marks a distinct break with the old. It is predominantly Marxist, more theoretical in orientation, and seeks to develop a much broader perception of Canada than any of its predecessors. Although still in its formative phase, it has already begun a significant reassessment of the broad economic and political issues which constitute Canadian historical reality. Such an undertaking is long overdue. There has been no major re-interpretation of Canadian history since the pioneering work of Innis and Creighton done in the thirties. Innis and Creighton saw the struggle for Canadian independence and the crises in national survival as the great themes in the making of Canada. The new political economy has returned to these basics, but with an entirely new focus. It has cut through much of the obfuscation and mythologizing of the basic issues by effectively applying dependency theory, class analysis, elite studies and contemporary models of capitalist development. The issues on its agenda are those of foreign ownership and capital accumulation, the branch plant economy and imperialism, modern technology and unequal development. It goes back to the politics of Confederation and Canada's internal national question, to the historical development of Canadian class structure and the nature of Canadian capitalism. In short, the new political economy establishes the basis for a new critical awareness of the forces that have shaped modern Canada.

R. T. Naylor is perhaps the most successful contributor to this revitalized movement in political economy. In a number of essays and a major study of commercial and industrial capital in the nineteenth and twentieth centuries, Naylor has undertaken a fundamental re-interpretation of Canadian history.[65] What the staple was to Innis, capital is to Naylor — the invisible tie that binds the Canadian periphery to the centre. With this new focus Naylor is able to show why Canadian capitalism in its formative period from the National Policy to World War I was unable to transcend its role as a raw materials supplier in the world economy and effect a transition to a fully developed industrial economy. Innis' answer had been that, within an imperial structure, the export of staples primes the industrial pump of the imperial economy, not Canada's. While retaining the idea of imperial blockage, Naylor deepens the analysis of the "staple trap" by seeing it as a product of dependent capitalist formation (particularly involving commercial-financial capital), and showing how this path led directly to a reliance on American industry with its entrepreneurship, patents, direct investment and branch plants.

Naylor singles out the role of the banks as pivotal in the transition of the Canadian economy. His basic argument is that the pattern of development — regionally, nationally and continentally — is tied directly to the activities of the banks, which influenced development in at least three ways, viz. by their unwillingness to finance nascent Canadian secondary industry, by deepening regional underdevelopment, for instance in the Maritimes and, most importantly, by their preference for financing the international movement of Canadian resources, particularly to the United States. It was these kinds of activities along with stock frauds, financial scandals, and the supplying of the New York money market with short-term funds which, Naylor forcefully argues, created a banking system "least suited to promoting industrial development in Canada."

The second part of the Naylor thesis explains how the Canadian economy did, in the end, undergo industrialization under a policy he calls "industrialization by invitation." What Naylor clearly shows is that this path to industrialization "reproduces the conservatism of commercial capitalism in a new guise, the development of inefficient non-innovative and backward industrial structures with a penchant for dependence on foreign technology, foreign capital and state assistance."[66] By the end of the National Policy the process of industrial dependency was in full swing. Foreign capital was gaining control of large sections of the most dynamic parts of the economy. By contrast, Canadian industrial enterprise with few exceptions remained small-scale and marginal, particularly in the manufacturing sectors of the second industrial revolution. In reconstructing the history of the period Naylor shows how the interests of an imperial ruling class, the Canadian state and the indigenous financial class (including a weak industrial sector) were linked together in a project of dependent industrialization, the unfolding of which we can still see before us today.

One of Naylor's major accomplishments is his undercutting of the principal myth of Canadian liberalism — the notion that a strategy of incremental growth based on foreign investment and the export of resources can generate a viable pattern of industrial development.[67]

What Naylor has done more successfully than anyone else is to expose the fallacy of this policy of mortgaging one's future. As he pointedly notes, "Dependence, like protection, is addictive. The very ease of access to British prtfolio investment and markets and to American direct investment and technology ensured a particular pattern of development culminating in the reinforcement of the principal weaknesses of the Canadian economy."[68] This is a far cry from any harmonious incremental growth towards industrial and economic maturity.

If Naylor advances our understanding of commercialism as one of the most pervasive forces in Canadian economic history, Stanley Ryerson's Unequal Union provides us with a seminal analysis of Canada's political development during part of its critically formative years.[69] Ryerson's work is the most successful attempt so far to develop a new historiography covering the period 1815-1880. It presents a coherent overview of the political, economic and cultural forces prior to and following Confederation, while focusing on two themes, "the interweaving of industrial capitalist development and the existence of two national communities of people."[70] Ryerson's starting point in this lucid study of the origins of modern Canada is the imprint of class on the shaping of the Confederation settlement.

By his development of these themes, Ryerson has restored to Canadian history an integral dimension which liberal historiography has systematically sought to eliminate. To Ryerson, Confederation had serious flaws built into it. It was a profoundly elitist, anti-democratic, imperial project, foisted on the population by a colonial business class. In effect Ryerson provides an analysis of the side of the Laurentian thesis that is implicit but never fully developed in Innis. Innis examined the mechanism of exploitation (the staple mode of production) but left the exploiters faceless and anonymous. In exploring and identifying the source of that exploitation, Ryerson is able to write a history which speaks of classes and national communities, industrialism and imperialism, and federalism and dependency as the crucial factors in the making of Canada from the aborted revolutions of 1837 through the Riel uprisings in the 1870s.

One of the reasons for Ryerson's importance is his ability to document the politics of the commercial elites, the so-called Fathers of Confederation. On the one hand, he says, the French Canadian nation is "given to understand that it is entering a partnership based on the principle of equality. On the other hand, it is accorded a state structure which embodies no such relationship. The much vaunted federalism is not that of a bi-national state; it is something else again. The optical illusion may persist, but the reality is different."[71] Ryerson explains why Confederation did not resolve or address itself in any significant way to Canada's internal national question. The Fathers of Confederation "evaded the bi-national reality because they conceived of a nation that reduced one of its parts to a religious and linguistic peculiarity, denying it an organic entity of nationhood by detaching the culture from its socio-economic being."[72]

For Ryerson the so-called duality of Canadian life is in reality the reflection of two peoples and two nations trapped in a political union which offered neither self-determination nor independence. It is Ryerson's contention that the political union which led to the founding of modern Canada came into existence in such a way that it offered no adequate basis for national survival for the people of either English or French

Canada.[73] He singles out three factors behind the idea of Confederation. He stresses that "the ruling bloc of social forces of the Canada of 1867...while capable of promoting capitalist enterprise, proved inadequate as a creator of national values or of democratic solidarity."[74] Secondly, "the collusion of the bourgeois-clerical French-Canadian leadership with Anglo-Canadian big business and the imperial power constituted a more potent force than the small middle-class national democratic and radical movement".[75] Finally, "the concept of the nation held by the men of property who had founded the new Dominion was coloured by their preoccupation with the 'cash nexus'. Nation-building was a huge transaction in real estate and railway company shares, an investor's challenge."[76]

Ryerson shares Innis' view of Confederation as an imperial project, what Innis dubbed a "cost accounting scheme" to protect British investments.[77] The Canadian elite and the colonial office had a mutual interest in the reorganization scheme which, it was believed, would bring a measure of stability and development to the northern half of the continent. But Ryerson's analysis of Confederation is telling us more than that. 1867 ushered in a period of home rule, a rather minor moment in the history of this turbulent period which speaks more than anything of the triumph of reaction and the corresponding defeat of the bourgeois democratic revolutions in English and French Canada. Ryerson is indeed on solid ground in claiming that the new state structure failed to provide the social or class basis for anything remotely resembling an independent nation. In time some of these features would come but as Ryerson states, the Confederation structures would be unequal to the task because they institutionalized inequality internally between French and English and among Central Canada, the Maritimes and the West, while providing none of the external conditions that would secure an independent binational state strong enough to withstand the economic forces that would eventually re-integrate Canada into a much stronger system of political domination.

Wallace Clement brings the analysis of Canada forward into the present from the perspective of sociology. Clement has moved far beyond Porter's narrow study by analyzing the point where class, elite interest and capitalist development intersect. In the most comprehensive examination of Canada's elites and elite structures to date, he addresses himself to two propositions: that the structure of elite power follows the flow of capital, and that the assimilation of a people begins with its leaders.

The launching pad for this inquiry, he tells us, is the proposition that two major processes have determined Canada's economic development in the post-war period. Between 1951 and 1972 there has been a marked tendency for an increasing centralization and concentration of capital into fewer and larger firms. These developments have allowed the economic elite to consolidate the avenues of access into its inner circles. Secondly, Clement shows that there has been an increasing penetration of the economy by foreign, especially American, direct investment which has given American interests control of key sectors of the economy. In both his major studies Clement proceeds to lay out an "erosion" model of elite power, showing the reason why the traditional elites in banking and commerce are able to expand and prosper from the very policies which led Canada into political dependency.

In The Canadian Corporate Elite, Clement demonstrates that power is divided unevenly among the foreign elite, who are the most powerful; the comprador elite, who manage and administer the branch plants; the parasitic elite, who control parent MNC's; and the indigenous elite, who own national corporations and who may or may not be linked with foreign corporations. In empirically delineating these relations, Clement has provided us with a map of elite power: who has power, who has lost it, how it is exercised and, the most important condition of holding power, how it is passed on. It is the latter point which Clement considers of paramount importance. The position of the elites depends upon their social connections and their economic interlocks. The study of the intricate web of family and school ties, shared company directorships, common ideological assumptions and positions of dominance in cultural institutions is one of the major themes in Clement's writings. But unlike others who have studied the elite, Clement insists that his sociological interest in the powerful is tied to the larger questions of class formation and capital accumulation, the central concerns of the new political economy.[78] It is in his second volume, Continental Corporate Power, that Clement brings these diverse themes together in a penetrating analysis of Canadian elite structure, economic power and the liberal ideology underpinning them.

By building on Naylor, Clement elucidates the paradox of elite economic activity, commercial growth and industrial decline. He demonstrates that, historically, Canadian development has always followed a commercial orientation, even after Canada entered an era of industrialism. He argues that this can only be explained by the fact that Canada's top capitalists, particularly the banks and the trust, insurance and mortgage companies, specialized in the sphere of circulation. "Given the easy movement into areas of production, the leading edge of Canada's capitalist class sought out and found foreign capitalists willing and able to enter the sphere of production in Canada."[79] The consequences of this mode of development were far-reaching. "Because Canadian capitalists specialized in circulation, they soon became dependent upon foreign capitalists in control of Canadian production."[80]

Clement argues that Canada's industrial revolution was necessarily incomplete, blocked by the twin forces of commercialism and imperialism. This takes him a considerable distance in uncovering the historic origins of Canadian dependency. On the one hand, Canada's most dynamic capitalists have turned to servicing United States capital, and on the other, "Canadian capitalists have clung to the initiative of foreign industrial capitalists as a surrogate for indigenous development."[81] It is this set of specific conditions, Clement maintains with great force, that creates an unequal alliance between Canada's financial capitalists and United States capital, with American MNC's in control of production in Canada and Canadian capitalists committed to servicing and expanding foreign control of the economy. "Thus the alliance, while unequal, represents a merging of efforts and interests, giving Canadian and U.S. capitalists an affinity."[82] It is the study of these affinity relationships, national and international, which lies at the heart of Clement's imaginative scholarship.

The pioneering works of Ryerson, Clement and Naylor constitute the beginnings of a major new statement in Canadian political economy. Their success is in no small measure due to the fact that Canadian political economy is now broadly based, with many individuals contributing to it. As well, the current revival reflects the reawakening of a national consciousness, which has pushed a new generation of political economists to question the orthodox structures of liberal social science. What has emerged from their collective efforts is a very different sense of Canada.

If there is one idea that stands in the forefront of their writing it is the condition that capital must be understood, above all, as a social relationship. This theoretical perspective has been the starting point for an examination of the long-run trends of two core issues, foreign ownership and foreign investment. Mel Watkins[83] has written extensively on the overall impact of foreign capital on Canadian development and makes the point that the Canadian economic process has been severely ruptured by these capital movements. Since the foreign investment is nowadays predominantly American and takes the form of direct investment, with the aim of giving the investor perpetual control of profits, foreign capitalists have had a major impact on the resource and manufacturing sectors of the economy. The distortions which result have created three related problems for Canada:

1. At the global level, Canada has experienced incomplete development with the result, as I have shown elsewhere,[84] of an unstable, hybrid form of capitalism, what may be termed "advanced resource capitalism." Canada is underindustrialized by imperial forces, though not to the point of being completely dependent, and it does of course share many of the social relationships of advanced capitalism found in Britain and the United States. The result is that Canada's status has regressed from that of a semi-centre economy to a semi-peripheral one.
2. At the continental level, underdevelopment, or what Laxer has termed de-industrialization,[85] occurs as a re-

sult of a blocking of indigenous growth by a variety of means including capital exports, balance of payments deficits, free trade agreements such as the Auto Pact and technology gaps.

3. At the regional level uneven development manifests itself as regional disparities caused by the long-term effects of resource mismanagement, out-migration, lack of local industrial development and high levels of unemployment.[86]

The crisis in "development" is symptomatic of the long-run effect of industrial decline. In the case of Canada these inefficiencies flow directly from the cumulative impact of state policy, as Bourgault has shown in the case of technology;[87] from the fragmenting of the domestic market by the presence of MNC's, as Levitt demonstrates;[88] from the crippling miniature replica effect on Canada's ability to exploit industrial goods, as documented by the Science Council[89] and Laxer and Laxer;[90] and from ill-conceived resources projects as shown by Pratt,[91] Dosman[92] and Watkins.[93] What the crisis in development points to is that Canada has become more like a dependent economy and less like a viable industrial country as it has regressed to a new stage of dependency in the last twenty-five years.

As Gonick has pointed out, this view of the economic crisis has a social dimension that affects Canada's political structures in a fundamental way.[94] The growth of regionalism, the spread of separatism in Quebec and the emergence of English-Canadian nationalism are visible responses to the crisis. These deep internal cleavages have now come to totally dominate the Canadian political landscape. What they reflect are national and class inequalities and the corrosive effects of marginalization. It is unlikely that these problems will move towards resolution in the short term. In these circumstances there will be more social unrest and upheaval rather than less.

A number of writers have adopted this general framework to study the social dynamics of the crisis. Milner and Milner[95] have explained Quebec nationalism and separatism in these terms; Paul Phillips,[96] Harold Chorney[97] and Bruce Archibald[98] have documented Maritime and Western regionalism from this perspective; Robert Laxer[99] and Cy Gonick[100] have discussed the implications of the crisis for the Canadian working class; Herschel Hardin[101] and Leo Panitch[102] et al. have examined different aspects of the state in mediating the crisis.

Yet despite this enormous intellectual output in the last five years the new political economy has not been able to produce a clearer synthesis of the development crisis. Writing in another context, Abraham Rotstein has made the important point that the crisis in Canada is mediated by the "astigmatism of liberal theory" which, he argues, is the "key to Canada's silent surrender":[103]

> Missing...was the internally rooted sense of a national self, that is, an independent political culture with its accompanying symbols to evoke and protect Canadian nationhood.
>
> What was thereby so effectively blotted out was the problem of power, particularly the locus of economic power. Thus, when power began to shift out of the Canadian economy to Chicago, New York and Washington by virtue of the highly visible and active hand of the multinational corporation, and by virtue of our dependence on Washington's legal and economic policies, we were barely conscious that anything of importance had happened. All we could ask was whether the "market" was functioning properly and whether

profits (something, anywhere) were being maximized.[104] This lack of a cultural self, or what I have termed deculturation, has also left its imprint on the resurgence of political economy, both in general and specific ways. Works that examine the national dimension of development, for instance, tend to be weak on the regional implications; studies that deal with Canada's internal dependence often ignore the national dimension; writers who focus on class frequently fail to acknowledge regional and/or external consequences; those who examine the economic side of dependence tend to be unaware of the cultural and social side of the issue, etc.

In terms of specifics, there are disquieting tendencies as well:

-an inability in much recent writing on political economy to explore common origins of Canada's external and internal national questions;

-a traditional predilection among the English-Canadian left to "discover" the central issue of foreign ownership and foreign domination and then during times of economic crises to ignore this aspect of Canadian political economy, letting it drop out of sight in favour of a Mackintoshite view of the world;[105]

-an unhealthy reliance on metropolitan models of Marxism to establish priorities, conceptual frameworks and research projects, which as past experience demonstrates is detrimental to the establishment of a Canadian Marxist tradition;

-a mistaken tendency to make an economic interpretation of Canadian development an end in itself.

There is an unfortunate absence of discussion on these important issues at present. Indeed, many political economists appear to be totally unaware of the extent to which liberal astigmatism has affected Canadian Marxism.

Dennis Lee has analyzed the same phenomenon in literature as writing in "colonial space."[106] What he describes is the painful realization that in a dependent culture voice and memory, the critical tools of thought and action are no more immediately accessible to the writer than they are to any other section of the population. To the degree that political economists share inherited colonial space, Lee's argument applies to them also. The point is that unless political economy faces up to its cultural and intellectual origins it will not acquire the maximum resonance at the theoretical, empirical and conceptual levels because, as part of its own development, it has failed to acquire an authenic voice and memory.

Political economy is not alone in this deformity. All Canadian social science suffers from it. Clearly, if the new political economy desires to tackle larger and more complex questions such as the role of the state in Canadian society, the class basis of Canada's social development and the nature of the Canadian political culture and ideology, it will have to deal with this condition of its origin as part of the process of moving forward.[107]

At this particular time there is an urgent need to force the pace of contextualizing Canadian political economy. When political economy addressed itself to this task in the past it was at its perceptive and analytical best. The need is no less urgent now.

Notes

1. For Innis' statement of the staple theory consult the conclusion of The Fur Trade in Canada (1930). For Mackintosh's, see his article "Economic Factors in Canadian History," in Easterbrook and Watkins, eds., Approaches to Canadian Economic History (1967). An amplification of Mackintosh's approach is found in his study done for the Rowell-Sirois Report, The Economic Background to Dominion-Provincial Relations (1938). These two should be read together for a comprehensive view of his theory of capitalist development.

2. The initial research on the statist tradition is found in Corry's much neglected study The Growth of Government Activities Since Confederation (1939). It was commissioned by the Rowell-Sirois Commission. Lower et al., Evolving Canadian Federalism (1943) brings together the views of Scott, Lower, etc., who played an important part in theorizing the post-reconstructionist phase of making the Canadian state an instrument of social policy. Scott's work, defending a centralized federalism, is particularly important in this regard. His writings are scattered and unfortunately have not been collected. See also P.E. Trudeau, Federalism and the French Canadians (1967). Forsey and others did much of the preliminary work on the state in Social Planning for Canada (1948) and many of their ideas became the social gospel of the state bureaucracy in the fifties.

3. See particularly K. Buckley, Capital Formation in Canada 1896-1930 (1955). Also Caves and Holton, The Canadian Economy (1959) and O.J. Firestone, Canada's Economic Development, 1867-1953 (1958).

4. For the cultural application, see M. McLuhan, The Mechanical Bride (1951). On the constitution, see J.R. Mallory, Social Credit and the Federal Power in Canada (1954). For the political aspect see C.B. Macpherson, Democracy in Alberta: Social Credit and the Party System (1953).

5. See S. Ryerson, Unequal Union (1968), and F. and L. Park, Anatomy of Big Business (1962).

6. See V. Fowke, The National Policy and the Wheat Economy (1957), G.E. Britnell, The Wheat Economy (1939), and S.A. Saunders' work done for the Rowell-Sirois Commission, Economic History of the Maritime Provinces (1939).

7. See. G. Teeple, ed., Capitalism and the National Question (1972), Kari Levitt, Silent Surrender (1970), T. Acheson, The Social Origins of Canadian Industrialism: A Study in the Structure of Entrepreneurship (1972), unpublished PhD. thesis, and R.T. Naylor's The History of Canadian Business, 1867-1914, Vols. I and II (1975).

8. See The Canadian Economy. In many respects their study is an impressive attempt to defend the Innis staple theory by constructing an econometric model of the Canadian economy. They also end up by watering down Innis' model of dependency.

9. For an early study see his Farm Credit in Canada (1937). For a sampling of his views on the philosophy of market forces see his article "Political Economy and Enterprise," CJEPS (August 1949). Easterbrook has chronicled the tradition in a bibliographic essay in Easterbrook and Watkins, eds., Approaches to Canadian Economic History (1967).

10. From Mary Q. Innis, ed., Essays in Canadian Economic History (1957), p. 405.

11. Easterbrook, in his wide-ranging bibliographic essay in Approaches, discusses the contributions to Canadian political economy but never comes to terms with what assumptions or principles sustained such a large body of academic research.

12. Included in this category are K. Taylor, B. Bryce, J. Deutsch, and W.C. Clarke. The deputy-ministers of finance have always been strongly continentalist in their approach to Canadian economic policy. Mackintosh was a key influence on the group.

13. For a useful overview of political economy, see C. Chattopadhyay, "Political Economy: What's in a Name?" Monthly Review (April 1974).

14. Ibid. It is hardly necessary here to review in detail the fact that there are large and unyielding differences between the two camps of political economy on this and other points. Compare for instance J.A. Schumpeter's The Theory of Economic Development (1934) with P. Baran and P. Sweezy, Monopoly Capital (1966), as illustrative of the chasm separating the two traditions.

15. Innis is a good example of the flexibility and diversity of political economy, working in three areas: the economy, the state, and culture. The more formal division of labour in social science is a fairly recent phenomenon. In the earlier period political economy was a meeting ground for social scientists from political science, economics, geography, and sociology.

16. See W.A. Mackintosh and W.L.G. Joerg, eds., Canadian Frontiers of Settlement, 9 vols. (1934-1940).

17. Academics chose to avoid this area of social inequality; others in Canada did not. See G. Myers, A History of Canadian Wealth (1914). One can also consult the Grain Growers Guide for populist research. Both the CCF and the Communist Party of Canada did research on this important question, publishing their findings in pamphlets and their own journals. The problem of monopoly and concentration did receive some attention, however fleeting. See, for example, L.G. Reynolds, The Control of Competition in Canada (1940), part of a series done in the Harvard Studies in Monopoly and Competition.

18. See Peter Pond: Fur Trader and Adventurer (1930), edited by Innis.

19. The question of imperialism and monopoly preoccupied Innis in his later writings, particularly the social consequences. For instance, he examines Americans at length in "Military Implications of the American Constitution," found in the final volume of his published writings, Changing Concepts of Time (1952). The entire volume is of great interest.

20. Canadian Marxists make the mistake of not reading the literature of Canadian liberal political economy. Its wealth of important historical research needs to be taken into consideration for their own writing. Too frequently it is dismissed out of hand. Instead, there needs to be a judicious sifting of this literature in preparation of new studies designed to tackle the unanswered questions contained in that legacy.

21. V. Bladen, From Adam Smith to Maynard Keynes: The Heritage of Political Economy (1975).

22. Macpherson is generally recognized as Canada's most distinguished Marxist scholar and yet his intellectual milieu remains very much part of British scholarship. As important as his contribution has been internationally, this does not take away from the fact that after his highly original work on Social Credit and the party system, his interest in Canadian studies came to an end. He himself has been a defender of Canadian political economy, although his interests continue to lie elsewhere.

23. A. Memmi, in The Colonizer and the Colonized (1965) says, "...the colonialist is unsure of his true nationality. He navigates between a faraway society which he wants to make his own (but which becomes to a certain degree mythical!), and a present society which he rejects and thus keeps in the abstract" (p. 68). M. Atwood, in Survival (1972), draws up a typology of "victim" positions. Social autism is most likely to occur in position one: "to deny the fact that you are a victim" (p. 36).

24. See Canada's Crisis in Higher Education, proceedings of a conference held by the National Conference of Canadian Universities (1956). The organizer was Claude Bissell, then president of Carleton University. Part of the funding came from the Ford and Rockefeller foundations. The model for reforming the university and upgrading Canadian social science was patterned after the work of Clark Kerr in the United States.

25. Done by myself as a member of the Committee on Canadian Content of the C.P.S.A. 1973, though not included in its report.

26. H. Neatby, So Little for the Mind (1952).

27. Lament for a Nation (1965).

28. Right and Wrong in Foreign Policy (1965).

29. Alan Cairns, "Political Science in Canada and the Americanization Issue," CJPS (June 1975). Donald Smiley, "Must Canadian Political Science Be a Miniature Replica?," Journal of Canadian Studies (1974).

30. For one of the more lucid statements summing up the perspective of the Laurentian school, see W.L. Morton's "Clio in Canada: The Interpretation of Canadian History" in Approaches to Canadian History, Volume 1 (1967).

31. See Empire of the St. Lawrence (1937).

32. The Progressive Party in Canada (1950).

33. A classic essay of Innis', illustrating the interaction between the "economic" and "social" forces, is "The Canadian Economy and the Depression" in Essays in Canadian Economic History (1957). It is in his writing on communications that this aspect of Innis' approach blossoms into full view.

34. Empire and Communications (1972), p. 5.

35. The Fur Trade in Canada (1930).

36. "Economic Factors," in Easterbrook, ed., Approaches, p. 4.

37. Ibid., p. 12.

38. Ibid., p. 15.

39. For a sampling of Underhill's early scholarship, consult In Search of Canadian Liberalism (1961). The promise of his early writing is not fulfilled in his later articles.

40. The Growth of Government Activities.

41. See his Pioneer Public Service: An Administrative History of the United Canadas, 1841-1867 (1955).

42. See note 2.

43. For a sample of Innis' later views, consult Changing Concepts of Time (1952).

44. American Capital and Canadian Resources (1961).

45. Buckley, Britnell, and Fowke were faculty at the University of Saskatchewan; Soward at UBC; Pentland at Manitoba.

46. See V. Fowke, The National Policy, and K. Buckley, Capital Formation.

47. See Social Credit and Democracy in Alberta respectively.

48. See The Mechanical Bride.

49. Ferns and Ostry, The Age of Mackenzie King (1955).

50. See his unpublished PhD. thesis, Labour and the Development of Industrial Capitalism in Canada, Toronto (1960). It has become an underground classic of Canadian political economy.

51. See Urban Development in South-Central Ontario (1972).

52. See Unequal Union and The Founding of Canada. Ryerson also published many shorter pieces in Horizons, a now defunct Marxist journal, as well as in National Affairs Monthly.

53. Democracy in Alberta, p. xii.

54. See The Mechanical Bride.

55. See chapter IV, "The Federal System Between the Wars."

56. See The Mechanical Bride.

57. Democracy in Alberta, p. 244.

58. Ibid., p. 249.

59. Ibid., p. 247.

60. Ibid., pp. 240-241.

61. See The Canadian Economy.

62. In Approaches to Canadian History (1967).

63. Brecher and Reisman's study, done for the Gordon Commission on Canada-U.S. relations, reflects the ambivalence of the new technique of post-Innisian economics as well as an attempt to retain some of Innis' essential insights. As one would expect, their study ends up with the worst possible combination. For instance, they cannot account for Canada's continued reliance on the United States for capital imports. Their own evidence shows that for the period 1948-1954, Canada is almost capital-sufficient. Why, then, is there a need to import capital? They do not relate this phenomenon to the imperialism of trade which forces Canada to cover its trade deficit by encouraging foreign investment. See also H. Johnson's review of the Gordon Commission in The Canadian Quandary (1963).

64. Canadian students in economics are often required to read The Fur Trade in Canada (1930). The way Innis is taught, however, is almost guaranteed to lead to an instant aversion. The stress is on the actual trade in furs. Of course, the fur trade is meant to symbolize the means of production and all the social relations which flow from this period of commerce. When this dimension of his work is forgotten and played down, it is not surprising that Innis can be made to appear a most pedantic economic historian.

65. See R.T. Naylor, "The Rise and Fall of the Third Commercial Empire of the St. Lawrence" in Capitalism and the National Question in Canada, edited by G. Teeple (1972); "Setting Naylor's Critics Straight" in Canadian Dimension (November 1974); The History of Canadian Business, 1867-1914, Vols. I and II; "Dominion of Capital: Canada and International Investment" in Domination, edited by A. Kontos (1976); and "Response to Ryerson" in This Magazine 11:3 (May-June 1977).

66. "Dominion of Capital," in A. Kontos, ed., Domination, p. 52.

67. See W.A. Mackintosh's classic study, The Economic Background to Dominion-Provincial Relations, vol. II.

68. The History of Canadian Business, Vol. II, p. 283.

69. Ryerson disagrees with aspects of Naylor's thesis of commercial versus industrial capital although he himself has shown, for the period prior to the National Policy, that a native bourgeoisie had suffered a severe setback in the defeat of the Rebellions of 1837 and by the time of Confederation had only partially recovered. See his review of Naylor's History (1975) in This Magazine 10:5-6 (November-December 1976). Unfortunately, Ryerson does not present us with his own interpretation of the issues which Naylor raises about the dependent nature of Canadian capitalism and Unequal Union (1968) does not cover the period of Naylor's analysis in any detail.

70. See Chapter 19, "French Canada and Terms of Union" in Unequal Union (1968).

71. Ibid., pp. 375-376.

72. Ibid., p. 376.

73. For a Quebec view of Confederation which elaborates this general point, see Alfred Dubuc's excellent article, "The Decline of Confederation and the New Nationalism" in Nationalism in Canada, edited by Peter Russell (1966); also Pierre Vallieres, White Niggers of America (1971).

74. Ryerson, Unequal Union, p. 240.

75. Ibid., p. 378.

76. Ibid., p. 422.

77. See H. Innis, Problems in Staple Production in Canada (1933).

78. For an analytical discussion of this question, see James Petras' valuable article, "New Perspectives on Imperialism and Social Classes in the Periphery" in Journal of Contemporary Asia 5:3 (1975).

79. W. Clement, Continental Corporate Power (1977), p. 17.

80. Ibid.

81. Ibid., p. 18.

82. Ibid., p. 6.

83. See his article, "The Staple Theory Revisited" in Papers of the Canadian Political Science Association (1976) and "Economic Development of Canada and the World Inequality" in World Inequality (1975) edited by I. Wallerstein.

84. D. Drache, "Staple-ization: A Theory of Canadian Capitalist Development" in Imperialism, Nationalism, and Canada (1977) edited by Craig Heron.

85. James Laxer, "Canadian Manufacturing and U.S. Trade Policy" in (Canada) Ltd. (1973) edited by Robert Laxer.

86. See Paul Phillips, "National Policy, Continental Economics, and National Disintegration" in Canada and the Burden of Unity (1977) edited by David Bercuson.

87. Innovation and the Structure of Canadian Industry, Science Council of Canada, Background Study, no. 23 (1972).

88. Silent Surrender: The Multinational Corporation in Canada (1970).

89. Uncertain Prospects: Canadian Manufacturing Industry 1971-1977 (1977).

90. James and Robert Laxer, The Liberal Idea of Canada (1977).

91. Larry Pratt, The Tar Sands (1976).

92. Edgar Dosman, The National Interest: Politics of Northern Development 1968-1975 (1976).

93. Mel Watkins, ed., Dene Nation: The Colony Within (1977).

94. See Inflation or Depression? (1976).

95. The Decolonization of Quebec (1973).

96. See his essay in Canada and the Burden of Unity.

97. "Regional Underdevelopment and Cultural Decay" in Imperialism, Nationalism, and Canada, op. cit.

98. "Atlantic Regional Underdevelopment and Socialism" in Essays on the Left (1971) edited by Laurier Lapierre.

99. Canada's Unions (1976).

100. See Inflation or Depression.

101. A Nation Unaware: Canadian Economic Culture (1974).

102. The Canadian State: Political Economy and Political Power (1977).

103. "Canada: The New Nationalism" in Foreign Affairs 55:1 (October 1976), p. 109.

104. Ibid.

105. See pp. 12-13 of the text.

106. "Cadence, Country, Silence: Writing in Colonial Space," Open Letter 2:6 (Fall 1973).

107. In this regard, Clement and I are carrying out a systematic study of class and the political economy tradition in Canada, the results of which will be published in late 1978.

BIBLIOGRAPHY

I. FACTORS OF DEVELOPMENT

1. RESOURCES AND STAPLES

Aitken, H.G.J.
American Capital and Canadian Resources. Cambridge, Mass.: Harvard University Press, 1961.

Berger, Thomas
Northern Frontier, Northern Homeland: The Report of the Mackenzie Valley Pipeline Inquiry. Ottawa: Supply and Services Canada, 1977.

Bocking, Richard C.
Canada's Water: For Sale? Toronto: James Lewis and Samuel, 1972.

Buckley, Kenneth
"The Role of the Staple Industries in Canada's Economic Development." Journal of Economic History 18:4 (December 1958):439-450.

Burley, Kevin H., ed.
The Development of Canada's Staples, 1867-1939: A Documentary Collection. The Carleton Library, no. 56. Toronto: McClelland and Stewart, 1971.

Canada. Department of Energy, Mines and Resources
An Energy Policy for Canada, Phase 1--Analysis. Ottawa: Queen's Printer, 1973.

Canada. Department of Energy, Mines and Resources
An Energy Policy for Canada. Ottawa: Queen's Printer, 1976.

Canada. Dominion Bureau of Statistics
Canadian Mineral Statistics, 1886-1956; Mining Events, 1604-1956. Reference Paper Number 68. Ottawa: Queen's Printer, 1957.

Canada. Royal Commission on Canada's Economic Prospects
Canadian Energy Prospects. Ottawa: Queen's Printer, 1957.

Canada. Royal Commission on Canada's Economic Prospects
The Outlook for the Canadian Forest Industries. Hull: Queen's Printer, 1957.

Canada. Science Council
Canada's Energy Opportunities. Report Number 23. Ottawa: Information Canada, 1975.

Caves, R.E., and Holton, R.H.
The Canadian Economy; Prospect and Retrospect. Harvard Economic Studies, vol. 112. Cambridge, Mass.: Harvard University Press, 1959.

Chalmers, J.W., and Eccles, W.J., eds.
Philip's Historical Atlas of Canada. London, Eng.: George Philip, 1966.

RESOURCES AND STAPLES (cont'd)

Clement, Wallace, and Janzen, Anna
"Just Peachy: The Demise of Tender Fruit Farmers." This Magazine 12:2 (May 1978):22-26.

Creighton, D.G.
Harold Adam Innis: Portrait of a Scholar. Toronto: University of Toronto Press, 1978. (First published 1957).

Crommelin, Michael
"Energy Sellout. A Counter-Report." Canadian Forum 53 (June-July 1973):6-7.

Denison, Merrill
The People's Power: The History of Ontario Hydro. Toronto: McClelland and Stewart, 1960.

Deverell, John, and The Latin American Working Group
Falconbridge: Portrait of a Canadian Mining Multinational. Toronto: James Lorimer, 1975.

Drache, Daniel
"Ten Good Years: The Beginnings of Hinterland Resistance." This Magazine 8:3 (August-September 1974):30-34.

"Canadian Capitalism: Sticking with Staples." This Magazine 9:3 (July-August 1975):7-10.

"Staple-ization: A Theory of Canadian Capitalist Development." Imperialism, Nationalism, and Canada, pp. 15-33. Edited by John Saul and Craig Heron. Toronto: New Hogtown Press, 1977.

Erickson, Edward W., and Waverman, Leonard, eds.
The Energy Question: An International Failure of Policy. 2 vol. Toronto: University of Toronto Press, 1974.

Forsey, Eugene
National Problems of Canada: Economic and Social Aspects of the Nova Scotia Coal Industry. McGill University Economic Studies, no. 5. Montreal: Macmillan, 1926.

"The Pulp and Paper Industry." Canadian Journal of Economics and Political Science 1:3 (1935):501-509.

Freeman, J.M.
Biggest Sellout in History: Foreign Ownership of Alberta's Oil and Gas Industry and the Oil Sands. Edmonton: Alberta N.D.P., 1966.

Galbraith, J.S.
The Hudson's Bay Company as an Imperial Factor, 1821-1869. Toronto: University of Toronto Press, 1957.

RESOURCES AND STAPLES (cont'd)

Gibbons, M. and Voyer, R.
A Technological Assessment System: A Case Study of East Coast Offshore Petroleum Exploration. Background Study No. 30. Ottawa: Science Council of Canada, March, 1974.

Gilchrist, John
"Exploration and Enterprise--The Newfoundland Fishery c. 1497-1677." Canadian Business History: Selected Studies, 1497-1971, pp. 7-26. Edited by D.S. Macmillan. Toronto: McClelland and Stewart, 1972.

Gray, Earle
The Great Canadian Oil Patch. Toronto: Maclean-Hunter, 1970.

Hann, Russell
Farmers Confront Industrialism: Some Historical Perspectives on Ontario Agrarian Movements. 3rd. rev. ed. Toronto: New Hogtown Press, 1975.

Hartland, Penelope
"Factors in Economic Growth in Canada." Journal of Economic History 15:1 (1955):13-22.

Higgins, Larratt
"The Alienation of Canadian Resources: The Case of the Columbia River Treaty." Close the 49th Parallel, Etc.: The Americanization of Canada, pp. 223-240. Edited by Ian Lumsden. Toronto: University of Toronto Press, 1970.

Hurlich, Susan
"Up Against the Bay: Resource Imperialism and Native Resistance." This Magazine 9:4 (September-October 1975):3-8.

Innis, Harold A.
Problems of Staple Production in Canada. Toronto: Ryerson Press, 1933.

"Significant Factors in Canadian Economic Development." Canadian Historical Review 18:4 (December 1937):374-384.

The Cod Fisheries: The History of an International Economy. Rev. ed. Toronto: University of Toronto, 1954. (First edition 1940).

The Fur Trade in Canada: An Introduction to Canadian Economic History. Rev. ed. Toronto: University of Toronto Press, 1956. (First edition 1930).

Essays in Canadian Economic History. Edited by Mary Q. Innis. Toronto: University of Toronto Press, 1956.

RESOURCES AND STAPLES (cont'd)

Innis, H.A., and Lower, A.R.M., eds.
Select Documents in Canadian Economic History, 1497-1783. Toronto: University of Toronto Press, 1929.

Innis, H.A., and Plumptre, A.F.W., eds.
The Canadian Economy and Its Problems. Toronto: University of Toronto Press, 1934.

Irvine, William
The Farmers in Politics. Toronto: McClelland and Stewart, 1976. (First published 1920).

Jenness, Diamond
The Indians of Canada. 7th ed. Toronto: University of Toronto Press, 1977.

Keith, Robert F.
Northern Development and Technology Assessment Systems: A Study of Petroleum Development Programs in the Mackenzie Delta-Beaufort Sea Region and the Arctic Islands. Background Study No. 34. Ottawa: Science Council of Canada, 1976.

Kierans, Eric
"The Kierans Report." Canadian Dimension 9:5 (May 1973):36-41.

"Canadian Resources Policy." Canadian Forum (June-July 1973): 56-63.

Report on Natural Resources Policy in Manitoba. Prepared for the Government of Manitoba. Winnipeg: Queen's Printer, 1973.

Kilbourn, William
Pipeline: TransCanada and the Great Debate, A History of Business and Politics. Toronto: Clarke, Irwin, 1970.

Laxer, James
The Energy Poker Game: The Politics of the Continental Resources Deal. Toronto: New Press, 1970.

Canada's Energy Crisis. Rev. ed. Toronto: James Lorimer, 1974.

Laxer, James, and Martin, Anne, eds.
The Big Tough Expensive Job: Imperial Oil and the Canadian Economy. Erin, Ont.: Press Porcepic, 1977.

LeBourdais, D.M.
Sudbury Basin: The Story of Nickel. Toronto: Ryerson Press, 1953.

RESOURCES AND STAPLES (cont'd)

Levere, Trevor H., and Jarrell, Richard A., eds.
A Curious Fieldbook: Science and Society in Canadian History. Toronto: Oxford University Press, 1974.

Lower, A.R.M.
The North American Assault on the Canadian Forest: A History of the Lumber Trade Between Canada and the United States. Toronto: Ryerson Press, 1938.

Great Britain's Wood Yard: British America and the Timber Trade, 1763-1867. Montreal: McGill-Queen's University Press, 1973.

"The Trade in Square Timber." Approaches to Canadian Economic History: A Selection of Essays, pp. 28-48. Edited by W.T. Easterbrook and M.H. Watkins. Toronto: McClelland and Stewart, 1967.

Lucas, Rex
Minetown, Milltown, Railtown: Life in Canadian Communities of a Single Industry. Toronto: University of Toronto Press, 1971.

Mackintosh, W.A.
"Economic Factors in Canadian History." Approaches to Canadian Economic History: A Selection of Essays, pp. 1-15. Edited by W.T. Easterbrook and M.H. Watkins. Toronto: McClelland and Stewart, 1967.

Macpherson, C.B.
Democracy in Alberta: Social Credit and the Party System. 2nd ed. Toronto: University of Toronto Press, 1968. (First edition 1953).

Main, O.D.
The Canadian Nickel Industry: A Study in Market Control and Public Policy. Canadian Studies in Economics, no. 4. Toronto: University of Toronto Press, 1955.

Mathias, Philip
Takeover: The 22 Days of Risk and Decision That Created the World's Largest Newsprint Empire, Abitibi-Price. Toronto: Maclean-Hunter, 1976.

McDougall, John
"Regulation Versus Politics: The National Energy Board and the Mackenzie Valley Pipeline." Continental Community? Independence and Integration in North America, pp. 250-273. Edited by A. Axline, et al. Toronto: McClelland and Stewart, 1974.

Mendels, M.M.
The Asbestos Industry of Canada. McGill University Economic Studies, no. 14. Montreal: McGill University, 1930.

RESOURCES AND STAPLES (cont'd)

Mitchell, Don
The Politics of Food. Toronto: James Lorimer, 1975.

Mitchell, Elaine Allan
Fort Timiskaming and the Fur Trade. Toronto: University of Toronto Press, 1977.

Moore, E.S.
American Influence in Canadian Mining. Political Economy series, no. 9. Toronto: University of Toronto Press, 1941.

Morrison, N.F.
Canadian Manufacturing Industries: A Study of the Localization of Canadian Secondary Industries. Toronto: Ryerson, 1937.

Nelles, H.V.
The Politics of Development: Forests, Mines and Hydro-Electric Power in Ontario, 1849-1941. Toronto: Macmillan, 1974.

O'Malley, Martin
The Past and Future Land: An Account of the Berger Inquiry Into the Mackenzie Valley Pipeline. Toronto: Peter Martin Associates, 1976.

Ontario. Advisory Committee on Energy
Energy in Ontario: The Outlook and Policy Implications. 2 vol. Toronto: Queen's Printer, 1972.

Ontario. Royal Commission on the Mineral Resources of Ontario
Report. Toronto: Queen's Printer, 1890.

den Otter, A.
"Social Life of a Mining Community: The Coal Branch." Alberta Historical Review 17:4 (Autumn 1969):1-11.

Pearse, Peter H., ed.
The Mackenzie Pipeline: Arctic Gas and Canadian Energy Policy. A Carleton Contemporary. Toronto: McClelland and Stewart, 1974.

Pratt, Larry
The Tar Sands: Syncrude and the Politics of Oil. Edmonton: Hurtig Publishers, 1976.

Prentice, Alison
The School Promoters: Education and Social Class in Mid-Nineteenth Century Upper Canada. Toronto: McClelland and Stewart, 1977.

Ray, Arthur J.
Indians in the Fur Trade: Their Role As Trappers, Hunters, and Middlemen in the Lands Southwest of Hudson Bay, 1660-1860. Toronto: University of Toronto Press, 1974.

RESOURCES AND STAPLES (cont'd)

Ray, Arthur J., and Freeman, Donald
'Give Us Good Measure': An Analysis of Hudson's Bay Company Post Accounts to 1763. Toronto: University of Toronto Press, 1978.

Reich, Nathan
National Problems of Canada: The Pulp and Paper Industry in Canada. McGill University Economic Studies, no. 7. Montreal: Macmillan, 1926.

Rich, E.E.
The Hudson's Bay Co., 1670-1870. 3 vols. Toronto: McClelland and Stewart, 1960.

"Trade Habits and Economic Motivation Among the Indians of North America." Canadian Journal of Economics and Political Science 26:1 (February 1960):35-53.

Richardson, Boyce
James Bay: The Plot to Drown the North Woods. Toronto: Clarke Irwin, 1973.

Ridgeway, James
The Last Play: The Struggle to Monopolize the World's Energy Resources. Toronto: Clarke Irwin, 1973.

Roseman, Frank, and Wilkinson, Bruce
"Who Benefits? The Alberta Energy Price Increases." Canadian Forum 53 (June-July 1973):48-52.

Scott, Anthony
Natural Resources: The Economics of Conservation. 2nd ed. The Carleton Library, no. 67. Toronto: McClelland and Stewart, 1973.

Sinclair, B.; Ball, N.R.; and Petersen, J.O., eds.
Let Us Be Honest and Modest: Technology and Society in Canadian History. Toronto: Oxford University Press, 1974.

Smith, Philip
Brinco: The Story of Churchill Falls. Toronto: McClelland and Stewart, 1975.

Stevenson, Garth
"Federalism and the Political Economy of the Canadian State." The Canadian State: Political Economy and Political Power, pp. 71-100. Edited by Leo Panitch. Toronto: University of Toronto Press, 1977.

Sykes, Philip
Sellout: The Giveaway of Canada's Energy Resources. Edmonton: Hurtig Publishers, 1973.

RESOURCES AND STAPLES (cont'd)

Warnock, Jack
"Potash in Saskatchewan: Keeping It Safe for the 'Multi-Nationals'." This Magazine 7:4 (January 1974):3-9.

Waterfield, Donald
Continental Waterboy: The Columbia River Controversy. Toronto: Clarke, Irwin, 1970.

Watkins, Mel
"A Staple Theory of Economic Growth." Canadian Journal of Economics and Political Science 29:2 (May 1963):141-158. Reprinted in Approaches to Canadian Economic History: A Selection of Essays, pp. 49-73. Edited by W.T. Easterbrook and Mel Watkins. Toronto: McClelland and Stewart, 1967.

"The Dismal State of Economics in Canada." Close the 49th Parallel, Etc.: The Americanization of Canada, pp. 197-208. Edited by Ian Lumsden. Toronto: University of Toronto Press, 1970.

"Resources and Underdevelopment." Canada Ltd.: The Political Economy of Dependency, pp. 107-208. Edited By Robert Laxer. Toronto: McClelland and Stewart, 1973.

"Economic Development in Canada." World Inequality: Origins and Perspectives, pp. 72-96. Edited by I. Wallerstein. Montreal: Black Rose Books, 1975.

"The Staple Theory Revisited." Canadian Political Science Association Papers 5 (May 1976):1-29.

Watkins, Mel, ed.
Dene Nation: The Colony Within. Toronto: University of Toronto Press, 1977.

(SEE ALSO: Class Formation)

2. FINANCE AND CAPITAL FORMATION

Aitken, Hugh G.J.
"A Note on the Capital Resources of Upper Canada." *Canadian Journal of Economics and Political Science* 18:4 (November 1952):525-533.

Beckhart, B.H.
The Banking System of Canada. New York: Holt, 1929.

Bertram, G.W.
"Economic Growth in Canadian Industry, 1870-1915: The Staple Model and the Take-Off Hypothesis." *Canadian Journal of Economics and Political Science* 29:2 (May 1963):159-184.

Bonin, B.
L'investissement étranger à long terme au Canada: ses caractères et effets sur l'économie canadienne. Problèmes économiques contemporains, no. 3. Montréal: Les Presses de l'Ecole des Hautes Etudes Commerciales, 1967.

Brecher, Irving
"The Flow of United States Investment Funds into Canada Since World War II." *The American Economic Impact on Canada*, pp. 100-126. Edited by H.G.J. Aitken, et al. Durham, N.C.: Duke University Press, 1959.

Monetary and Fiscal Thought and Policy in Canada, 1919-1939. Canadian Studies in Economics, no. 8. Toronto: University of Toronto Press, 1957.

Brecher, Irving, and Reisman, S.S.
Canada-United States Economic Relations: The Royal Commission on Canada's Economic Prospects. Ottawa: Queen's Printer, 1957.

Buckley, Kenneth
Capital Formation in Canada, 1896-1930. The Carleton Library, no. 77. Toronto: McClelland and Stewart, 1970. (First published 1955).

Caves, R.E., and Reuber, G.L.
Canadian Economic Policy and the Impact of International Capital Flows. Canada in the Atlantic Economy, no. 10. Toronto: University of Toronto Press, 1969.

Comité interministeriel sur les investissements étrangers
Rapport sur les investissements étrangers. (Rapport Tetley). Quebec: Queen's Printer, 1974.

Denison, Merrill
Canada's First Bank: A History of the Bank of Montreal. 2 vol. Montreal: McClelland and Stewart, 1966-1967.

FINANCE AND CAPITAL FORMATION (cont'd)

Drummond, Ian M.
"Canadian Life Insurance Companies and the Capital Market, 1890-1914." Canadian Journal of Economics and Political Science 28:2 (May 1962):204-224.

Field, F.W.
Capital Investments in Canada: Some Facts and Figures Respecting One of the Most Attractive Investment Fields in the World. 2nd ed. Montreal: Monetary Times of Canada, 1914. (First edition 1911).

Hammond, Bray
"Banking in Canada Before Confederation, 1792-1867." Approaches to Canadian Economic History: A Selection of Essays, pp. 127-168. Edited by W.T. Easterbrook and M.H. Watkins. Toronto: McClelland and Stewart, 1967.

Hartland, Penelope
"Canada's Balance of Payments Since 1868." Trends in the American Economy in the 19th Century, pp. 717-755. Princeton: Princeton University Press, 1960.

"Factors in Economic Growth in Canada." Journal of Economic History 15:1 (March 1955):13-22.

Hood, W.C., and Scott, A.
Output and Capital in the Canadian Economy. Royal Commission on Canada's Economic Prospects. Ottawa: Queen's Printer, 1957.

Macdonald, Larry
"Merchants Against Industry: An Idea and Its Origins." Canadian Historical Review 56:3 (September 1975):263-281.

Masters, D.C.
"Toronto Versus Montreal: The Struggle for Financial Hegemony, 1860-1875." Canadian Historical Review 22:2 (June 1941):133-146.

McBride, Steve
"Setting Naylor Straight." Canadian Dimension 10:2 (June 1974): 2, 56.

McIvor, R.C.
Canadian Monetary, Banking and Fiscal Development. Toronto: Macmillan, 1958.

Myers, Gustavus
A History of Canadian Wealth. 1st Canadian ed. Toronto: James, Lewis and Samuel, 1972. (First published 1914).

FINANCE AND CAPITAL FORMATION (cont'd)

Naylor, R.T.

"The Rise and Fall of the Third Commercial Empire of the St. Lawrence." Capitalism and the National Question in Canada, pp. 1-41. Edited by G. Teeple. Toronto: University of Toronto Press, 1972.

The History of Canadian Business, 1867-1914. 2 vol. Toronto: James Lorimer, 1975.

"Dominion of Capital: Canada and International Investment." Domination, pp. 33-56. Edited by A. Kontos. Toronto: University of Toronto Press, 1975.

"Response to Ryerson." This Magazine 11:3 (May-June 1977):32-33.

Neufeld, E.P., ed.

Money and Banking in Canada: Historical Documents and Commentary. The Carleton Library, no. 17. Toronto: McClelland and Stewart, 1964.

The Financial System of Canada: Its Growth and Development. Toronto: Macmillan, 1972.

Park, Libbie, and Park, Frank

Anatomy of Big Business. Toronto: James, Lewis and Samuel, 1973. (First published 1962).

Paterson, D.G.

"European Financial Capital and British Columbia: An Essay on the Role of the Regional Entrepreneur." BC Studies 21 (Spring 1974):33-47.

Pentland, H.C.

"The Role of Capital in Canadian Economic Development Before 1875." Canadian Journal of Economics and Political Science 16:4 (November 1950):457-474.

"Further Observations on Canadian Development." Canadian Journal of Economics and Political Science 19:3 (August 1953):403-410.

"Physical Productivity in Canada, 1935-52." Economic Journal 64 (June 1954):399-404.

Perry, J. Harvey

Taxes, Tariffs, and Subsidies: A History of Canadian Fiscal Development. 2 vol. Toronto: University of Toronto Press, 1955.

Pickett, James

"Residential Capital Formation in Canada, 1871-1921." Canadian Journal of Economics and Political Science 29:1 (Fall 1963):40-58.

FINANCE AND CAPITAL FORMATION (cont'd)

Ross, V.
A History of the Canadian Bank of Commerce. Vols. 1 and 2. Toronto: Oxford University Press, 1920-34.

Ryerson, Stanley
"Who's Looking After Business: A Review." This Magazine 10:5-6 (November-December 1976):41-46.

Shortt, A., and Doughty, A.G., eds.
A History of the Canadian People and Their Institutions. Canada and Its Provinces, vol. 10. Toronto: Glasgow, Brook & Co., 1914.

Stelter, G.A.
"Community Development in Toronto's Commercial Empire: The Industrial Towns of the Nickel Belt, 1883-1931." Laurentian University Review 6:3 (June 1974):3-53.

Swift, Jamie
The Big Nickel: INCO at Home and Abroad. Kitchener: Between the Lines, 1977.

Trigge, A.
A History of the Canadian Bank of Commerce: Vol. III, 1919-1930. Toronto: The Canadian Bank of Commerce, 1934.

Viner, Jacob
Canada's Balance of International Indebtedness, 1900-1913: An Inductive Study in the Theory of International Trade. The Carleton Library, no. 86. Toronto: McClelland and Stewart, 1975. (First published 1924).

Walker, David F., and Baker, James H.
Industrial Development in Southern Ontario: Selected Essays. Dept. of Geography, Publication series, no. 3. Waterloo: University of Waterloo, 1974.

Watkins, Mel
"Ryerson on Naylor: The Usefulness of Book Reviews." This Magazine 11:1 (January-February 1977):34.

Young, J.
Canadian Commercial Policy. Royal Commission on Canada's Economic Prospects. Ottawa: Queen's Printer, 1957.

(SEE ALSO: Multinationals, Branch Plants, and Canada AND Class Conflict)

3. INDUSTRIALIZATION

Acheson, T.W.
"The Social Origins of the Canadian Industrial Elite, 1880-1885." Canadian Business History, Selected Studies, 1497-1971, pp. 144-174. Edited by D.S. Macmillan. Toronto: McClelland and Stewart, 1972.

"Changing Social Origins of the Canadian Industrial Elite, 1880-1910." Business History Review 47:2 (Summer 1973):189-217.

Aitken, H.G.J.
The Welland Canal Company: A Study in Canadian Enterprise. Studies in Entrepreneurial History. Cambridge, Mass.: Harvard University Press, 1954.

Ashley, C.A.
The First Twenty-Five Years: A Study of Trans-Canada Air Lines. Toronto: Macmillan, 1963.

Bailey, A.G.
"Railways and the Confederation Issue in New Brunswick, 1863-1865." Culture and Nationality, pp. 76-92. The Carleton Library, no. 58. Toronto: McClelland and Stewart, 1972.

Berton, Pierre
The National Dream: The Great Railway, 1871-1881. Toronto: McClelland and Stewart, 1970.

Bertram, G.W.
"Economic Growth in Canadian Industry, 1870-1915: The Staple Model and the Take-Off Hypothesis." Canadian Journal of Economics and Political Science 29:2 (May 1963):159-184.

"Historical Statistics on Growth and Structure of Manufacturing in Canada, 1870-1957." Canadian Political Science Association Conference on Statistics: 1962 and 1963 Papers, pp. 13-151. Edited by J. Henripin and A.A. Asimakopulos. Toronto: University of Toronto Press, 1964.

Bladen, Vincent W.
"The Size of the Establishment in Canadian and American Industry." Contributions to Canadian Economics I (1928):56-68.

Bliss, Michael
A Living Profit: Studies in the Social History of Canadian Business, 1883-1911. Canadian Social History. Toronto: McClelland and Stewart, 1974.

Bourgault, Pierre
Innovation and the Structure of Canadian Industry. Science Council of Canada. Ottawa: Information Canada, October, 1972.

INDUSTRIALIZATION (cont'd)

Brewis, T.N., ed.
Growth and the Canadian Economy. The Carleton Library, no. 39. Toronto: McClelland and Stewart, 1968.

Canada. Department of Consumer and Corporate Affairs
Concentration in Manufacturing. Ottawa: Queen's Printer, 1971.

Carruthers, George
Paper-Making. Toronto: Garden City Press Co-operative, 1947.

Chodos, Robert
The CPR: A Century of Corporate Welfare. Toronto: James, Lewis and Samuel, 1973.

Chodos, Robert, and Burgess, Drummond
"Ma Bell Joins the Jet Set." Let Us Prey, pp. 33-49. Edited by Robert Chodos and Rae Murphy. Toronto: James Lorimer, 1974.

Clark, S.D.
The Canadian Manufacturers' Association: A Study in Collective Bargaining and Political Pressure. Toronto: University of Toronto Press, 1939.

Conway, G.R.
The Supply of and Demand for Canadian Equities. Toronto: Toronto Stock Exchange, Statistical Section, 1968.

Dales, John Harkness
Hydroelectricity and Industrial Development: Quebec, 1898-1940. Studies in Economic History. Cambridge, Mass.: Harvard University Press, 1957.

"Estimates of Canadian Manufacturing Output by Markets, 1870-1915." Canadian Political Science Association Conference on Statistics: 1962 and 1963 Papers, pp. 61-91. Edited by J. Henripin and A. Asimakopulos. Toronto: University of Toronto Press, 1964.

The Protective Tariff in Canada's Development: Eight Essays on Trade and Tariffs When Factors Move with Special Reference to Canadian Protectionism 1870-1955. Canadian University Paperbacks, no. 58. Toronto: University of Toronto Press, 1966.

Denison, Merrill
The Barley and the Stream: The Molson Story. Toronto: McClelland and Stewart, 1955.

Donald, W.J.A.
The Canadian Iron and Steel Industry: A Study in the Economic History of a Protected Industry. Income and Wealth, ser. 7. Boston: Houghton Mifflin, 1915.

INDUSTRIALIZATION (cont'd)

English, H.E.
"The Canadian Industrial Structure: An Essay on Its Nature and Efficiency." Contemporary Canada, pp. 81-103. Edited by Richard H. Leach. Toronto: University of Toronto Press, 1968.

Firestone, O.J.
Canada's Economic Development, 1867-1953, with Special Reference to Changes in the Country's National Product and National Wealth. Income and Wealth, ser. 7. London: Bowes and Bowes, 1958.

Forsey, Eugene
"Some Notes on the Early History of Unions in P.E.I." Canadian Historical Review 46:4 (December 1965):346-351.

Fullerton, D.H., and Hampson, H.A.
Canadian Secondary Manufacturing Industry. Hull, Que.: Queen's Printer, 1957.

Gilmour, James M.
Spatial Evolution of Manufacturing: Southern Ontario, 1851-1891. Dept. of Geography. Research Publications, no. 10. Toronto: University of Toronto Press, 1972.

Glazebrook, G.P. deT.
A History of Transportation in Canada. 2nd ed. 2 vol. The Carleton Library, no. 11-12. Toronto: McClelland and Stewart, 1964.

Grant, G.P.
Technology and Empire: Perspectives on North America. Toronto: House of Anansi, 1969.

Green, Alan G.
"Regional Aspects of Canada's Economic Growth, 1890-1929." Canadian Journal of Economics and Political Science 33:2 (May 1967): 232-245.

Guthrie, John Alexander
The Newsprint Paper Industry: An Economic Analysis. Harvard Economic Studies, vol. 68. Cambridge, Mass.: Harvard University Press, 1941.

Hann, Russell
Farmers Confront Industrialism: Some Historical Perspectives on Ontario Agrarian Movements. 3rd rev. ed. Toronto: New Hogtown Press, 1975.

Hartland, Penelope
"Factors in Economic Growth in Canada." Journal of Economic History 15:1 (1955):13-22.

INDUSTRIALIZATION (cont'd)

Hedley, Max J.
"Independent Commodity Production and the Dynamics of Tradition." Canadian Review of Sociology and Anthropology 13:4 (November 1976): 413-421.

Innis, H.A.
A History of the Canadian Pacific Railway. Toronto: McClelland and Stewart, 1923.

"Transportation as a Factor in Canadian Economic History." Papers and Proceedings of the Canadian Political Science Association. 3 (May 1931):166-184.

Johnson, Leo A.
"Land Policy, Population Growth and Social Structure in the Home District, 1793-1851." Ontario History 63:1 (March 1971):41-60.

Jones, Robert Leslie
History of Agriculture in Ontario, 1613-1880. University of Toronto Studies. History and Economics series, vol. 11. Toronto: University of Toronto Press, 1946.

Kilbourn, William
The Elements Combined: A History of the Steel Company of Canada. Toronto: Clarke, Irwin, 1960.

Knowles, L.C.A.
The Economic Development of the British Overseas Empire. London School of Economics and Political Science. Studies in Economics and Political Science. 2nd rev. ed., 2 vol. London: G. Routledge & Sons, 1928-36.

Lukasiewicz, J.
The Railway Game. A Carleton Contemporary. Toronto: McClelland and Stewart, 1976.

Macmillan, David S., ed.
Canadian Business History: Selected Studies, 1497-1971. Toronto: McClelland and Stewart, 1972.

Maddison, A.
"Productivity in Canadian Manufacturing (1935-1948)." Canadian Journal of Economics and Political Science 19:2 (May 1953):222-226.

Marshall, Herbert; Southard, Frank; and Taylor, Kenneth W.
Canadian-American Industry: A Study in International Investment. The Carleton Library, no. 93. Toronto: McClelland and Stewart, 1976. (First published 1936).

Masters, D.C.
The Rise of Toronto, 1850-1890. Toronto: University of Toronto Press, 1947.

McCalla, Douglas
"The Commercial Politics of the Toronto Board of Trade, 1850-60." Canadian Historical Review 50:1 (March 1969):51-67.

McDiarmid, O.J.
"Some Aspects of the Canadian Automobile Industry." Canadian Journal of Economics and Political Science 6:2 (May 1940):258-274.

Nelles, H.V.
The Politics of Development: Forest, Mines and Hydro-Electric Power in Ontario, 1840-1941. Toronto: Macmillan, 1974.

Neufeld, E.P.
A Global Corporation: A History of the International Development of Massey-Ferguson Limited. Toronto: University of Toronto Press, 1969.

Ontario. Department of Economics
A Century of Industrial Development in Ontario. Toronto: Queen's Printer, 1965.

Pentland, H.C.
"The Development of a Capitalistic Labour Market in Canada." Canadian Journal of Economics and Political Science 25:4 (November 1959):450-461.

Phillips, W.G.
The Agricultural Implement Industry in Canada: A Study of Competition. Canadian Studies in Economics, no. 7. Toronto: University of Toronto Press, 1956.

Plewman, William Rothwell
Adam Beck and the Ontario Hydro. Toronto: Ryerson Press, 1947.

Porritt, Edward
Sixty Years of Protection in Canada, 1846-1907: Where Industry Leans on the Politician. Toronto: Macmillan, 1908.

Porter, Glenn, and Cuff, Robert D., eds.
Enterprise and National Development: Essays in Canadian Business and Economic History. Toronto: Hakkert, 1973.

Rosenbluth, G.
Concentration in Canadian Manufacturing Industries. National Bureau of Economic Research: General Series, no. 61. Princeton: Princeton University Press, 1957.

INDUSTRIALIZATION (cont'd)

Rosenbluth, G.
"Concentration and Monopoly in the Canadian Economy." Social Purpose for Canada, pp. 198-248. Edited by M. Oliver. Toronto: University of Toronto Press, 1961.

Ryerson, Stanley
Unequal Union: Confederation and the Roots of Conflict in the Canadas, 1815-1873. Toronto: Progress Books, 1968.

The Founding of Canada. 2nd ed. Toronto: Progress Books, 1975. (First published 1960).

Safarian, E.A.
The Canadian Economy in the Great Depression. The Carleton Library, no. 54. Toronto: McClelland and Stewart, 1970. (First published 1959).

Skelton, Oscar D.
The Railway Builders, A Chronicle of Overland Highways. The Chronicles of Canada, vol. 32. Toronto: Glasgow, Brook, 1921. (First published 1916).

Spelt, Jacob
Urban Development in South-Central Ontario. The Carleton Library, no. 57. Toronto: McClelland and Stewart, 1972. (First published 1955).

Stevens, George Roy
Canadian National Railways. 2 vol. Toronto: Clarke, Irwin, 1960, 1962.

Travers, T.C.
"The Political Economy of Canadian Manufacturing, 1918-1931." PhD. thesis, York University, 1975.

Vaughn, W.
Sir William Van Horne. Toronto: Oxford University Press, 1926.

Warnock, Jack
"Free Trade Fantasies: The Case of the Farm Implements Industry." This Magazine 9:5-6 (November-December 1975):36-40.

"The Political Economy of the Food Industry in Canada: Oligopoly and American Domination." Our Generation 11:4 (Winter 1976):52-72.

Weldon, J.C.
"Consolidations in Canadian Industry, 1900-19." Restrictive Trade Practices in Canada: Selected Readings, pp. 228-279. Edited by L.A. Skeoch. Toronto: McClelland and Stewart, 1966.

INDUSTRIALIZATION (cont'd)

Williams, Glen
"Canadian Industrialization: We Ain't Growin' Nowhere." This Magazine 9:1 (March-April 1975):7-9.

Willoughby, William
The St. Lawrence Waterway: A Study in Politics and Diplomacy. Madison, Wisc.: University of Wisconsin Press, 1961.

Young, Brian J.
Promoters and Politicians: The North-Shore Railways in the History of Quebec, 1854-1885. Toronto: University of Toronto Press, 1978.

(SEE ALSO: Canada-United States Relations AND Multinationals, Branch Plants, and Canada)

II. FACTORS OF DEPENDENCY

1. IMPERIALISM

Amin, Samir

Accumulation on a World Scale: A Critique of the Theory of Underdevelopment. 2 vol. New York: Monthly Review Press, 1974.

Unequal Development: An Essay on the Social Formations of Peripheral Capitalism. New York: Monthly Review Press, 1976.

Baran, Paul A.

The Political Economy of Growth. 2nd ed. New York: Prometheus, 1962.

"On the Political Economy of Backwardness." The Political Economy of Development and Underdevelopment, pp. 82-93. Edited by Charles K. Wilber. New York: Random House, 1973.

Baran, Paul, and Sweezy, Paul

Monopoly Capital: An Essay on the American Economic and Social Order. New York: Monthly Review Press, 1966.

"Notes on the Theory of Imperialism." Readings in U.S. Imperialism, pp. 69-84. Edited by K.T. Fann and Donald C. Hodges. Boston: Porter Sargent, 1971.

Barnet, Richard J., and Muller, Ronald E.

Global Reach: The Power of the Multinational Corporations. New York: Simon and Schuster, 1974.

Barratt-Brown, Michael

The Economics of Imperialism. Penguin Modern Economics Texts. Harmondsworth: Penguin, 1974.

Behrman, J.N.

National Interests and the Multinational Enterprise: Tensions Among the North Atlantic Countries. Englewood Cliffs, N.J.: Prentice-Hall, 1970.

Block, Fred

"Expanding Capitalism: The British and American Cases." Berkeley Journal of Sociology 15 (1970):138-165.

Britnell, G.

"Underdeveloped Countries in the World Economy." Canadian Journal of Economics and Political Science 23:4 (November 1957):453-466.

Cardoso, F.H.

"Dependency and Development in Latin America." New Left Review 74 (July-August 1972):83-95.

IMPERIALISM (cont'd)

Chilicote, R.H.

"Dependency: A Critical Synthesis of the Literature." Latin American Perspectives 1:1 (Spring 1974):4-29.

Dos Santos, Theotonio

"The Changing Structure of Foreign Investment in Latin America." Latin America: Reform or Revolution?, pp. 94-98. Edited by J. Petras and M. Zeitlin. Greenwich, Conn.: Fawcett Publications, 1968.

"The Structure of Dependence." Readings in U.S. Imperialism. Edited by K.T. Fann and Donald C. Hodges. Boston: Porter Sargent, 1971.

"The Crisis of Development Theory and the Problem of Dependence in Latin America." Underdevelopment and Development, pp. 57-80. Edited by H. Bernstein. Harmondsworth: Penguin, 1973.

Engler, Robert

The Politics of Oil: A Study of Private Power and Democratic Directions. New York: Macmillan, 1961.

Fann, K.T., and Hodges, Donald C., eds.

Readings in U.S. Imperialism. Boston: Porter Sargent, 1971.

Fossum, Egil

"Political Development and Strategies for Change." Journal of Peace Research 7 (1970):17-32.

Frank, Andre Gunder

Latin America: Underdevelopment or Revolution. New York: Monthly Review Press, 1969.

Capitalism and Underdevelopment in Latin America: Historical Studies of Chile and Brazil. Rev. and enl. New York: Monthly Review Press, 1969.

"The Development of Underdevelopment." Latin America: Underdevelopment or Revolution, pp. 3-17. Edited by A.G. Frank. New York: Monthly Review Press, 1969.

"Sociology of Development and Underdevelopment of Sociology." Dependence and Underdevelopment, pp. 321-397. Edited by James D. Cockroft, et al. New York: Peter Smith, 1974.

"Who is the Immediate Enemy?" Dependence and Underdevelopment, pp. 425-433. Edited by James D. Cockroft, et al. New York: Peter Smith, 1974.

IMPERIALISM (cont'd)

Frank, Andre Gunder
Lumpenbourgeoisie: Lumpendevelopment. New York: Monthly Review Press, 1972.

"Dependence Is Dead: Long Live Dependence and the Class Struggle: An Answer to Critics." Latin American Perspectives 1:1 (Spring 1974):87-106.

Furtado, Celso
"The Concept of External Dependence in the Study of Underdevelopment." The Political Economy of Development and Underdevelopment, pp. 118-123. Edited by Charles K. Wilber. New York: Random House, 1973.

"Elements of a Theory of Underdevelopment--the Underdeveloped Structures." Underdevelopment and Development, pp. 33-43. Edited by H. Bernstein. Harmondsworth: Penguin, 1973.

Herzog, P.
Politique économique et planification en régime capitaliste. Editions sociales. Paris: Editions Sociales, 1971.

Hobsbawm, Eric J.
Industry and Empire. Harmondsworth: Penguin, 1969.

Horowitz, David
From Yalta to Vietnam: American Foreign Policy in the Cold War. Rev. ed. Harmondsworth: Penguin, 1967.

Horowitz, David, ed.
Corporations and the Cold War. New York: Monthly Review Press, 1969.

Hudson, Michael
Super Imperialism: The Economic Strategy of American Empire. New York: Holt, Rinehart and Winston, 1972.

Hymer, Stephen
"The Multinational Corporation and the Law of Uneven Development." Economics and World Order From the 1970's to the 1990's, pp. 113-140. Edited by J.N. Bhagwati. Toronto: Collier-Macmillan, 1972.

"The Efficiency (Contradictions) of Multinational Corporations." The Multinational Firm and the Nation State, pp. 49-65. Edited by Gilles Paquet. Toronto: Collier-Macmillan Canada, 1972.

"The Multinational Corporation: Your Home is Our Home." Canadian Dimension 8:6 (March-April 1972):29-32.

IMPERIALISM (cont'd)

Hymer, Stephen, and Rowthorn, Robert
"Multinational Corporations and International Oligopoly: The Non-American Challenge." The International Corporation: A Symposium, pp. 57-91. Edited by Charles Kindleberger. Cambridge, Mass.: MIT Press, 1970.

Islam, Nural
Foreign Capital and Economic Development: Japan, India and Canada. Rutland, Vt.: C.E. Tuttle, 1960.

Jalée, P.
The Pillage of the Third World. New York: Monthly Review Press, 1970.

The Third World in World Economy. New York: Monthly Review Press, 1969.

Imperialism in the Seventies. New York: Third Press, 1972.

Jenkins, Robin
Exploitation: The World Power Structure and the Inequality of Nations. London: Paladin, 1971.

Kautsky, Karl
"Ultra-Imperialism." New Left Review 59 (January-February 1970): 41-46.

Kay, Geoffrey
Development and Underdevelopment: A Marxist Analysis. New York: St. Martin's Press, 1975.

Kemp, T.
"The Marxist Theory of Imperialism." Studies in the Theory of Imperialism, pp. 15-34. Edited by Roger Owen and Bob Sutcliffe. New York: Longman, 1972.

Kiernan, E. Victor Gordon
Marxism and Imperialism. London: Edward Arnold, 1974.

Kindleberger, Charles, ed.
The International Corporation: A Symposium. Cambridge, Mass.: MIT Press, 1970.

Kolko, Gabriel
Politics of War: The World and United States Foreign Policy, 1943-45. New York: Random House, 1968.

Laclau, Ernesto
"Feudalism and Capitalism in Latin America." New Left Review 67 (May-June 1971):19-38.

LaFeber, Walter
America, Russia and the Cold War, 1945-1971. 2nd ed. New York: Wiley, 1972. (First edition 1968).

Lenin, V.I.
Imperialism, the Highest Stage of Capitalism. Peking: Foreign Languages Press, 1969. (First edition, 1917).

Lewis, Cleona
America's Stake in International Investments. Washington, D.C.: Brookings Institution, 1938.

Magdoff, H.
The Age of Imperialism: The Economics of U.S. Foreign Policy. New York: Monthly Review Press, 1969.

"Militarism and Imperialism." Readings in U.S. Imperialism, pp. 127-138. Edited by K.T. Fann and D.C. Hodges. Boston: Porter Sargent, 1971.

"Imperialism Without Colonies," Studies in the Theory of Imperialism, pp. 144-170. Edited by Roger Owen and Bob Sutcliffe. New York: Longman, 1972.

Mandel, Ernest
"The Laws of Uneven Development." New Left Review 59 (January-February 1970):19-38.

Marxist Economic Theory. London: Merlin Press, 1968.

Nicolaus, Martin
"The Universal Contradiction." New Left Review 59 (January-February 1970):3-18.

Nurkse, Ragnar
Problems of Capital Formation in Underdeveloped Countries, and Patterns of Trade and Development. A Galaxy Book, GB 181. New York: Oxford University Press, 1967.

O'Connor, Harvey
World Crisis in Oil. New York: Monthly Review Press, 1962.

"Inflation, Fiscal Crisis, and the American Working Class." Socialist Revolution No. 8, vol. 2:2 (March-April 1972):9-46.

Ogelsby, J.C.M.
Gringos from the Far North: Essays in Canadian-Latin American Relations. Toronto: Macmillan, 1975.

IMPERIALISM (cont'd)

Owen, Robert, and Sutcliffe, Bob, eds.
Studies in the Theory of Imperialism. New York: Longman, 1972.

Pailloix, C.
Les firmes multi-nationales et le procès d'internationalisation. Paris: Maspero, 1973.

Piel, J.
"The Current Role of the Nation-State." World Inequality: Origins and Perspectives, pp. 98-111. Edited by I. Wallerstein. Montreal: Black Rose Books, 1975.

Poulantzas, N.
Classes in Contemporary Capitalism. London: NLB, 1975.

Rowthorn, R., and Hymer, S.
International Big Business, 1957-1967: A Study of Comparative Growth. Cambridge, Eng.: University Press, 1971.

Schonfield, Andrew
Modern Capitalism: The Changing Balance of Public and Private Power. London: Oxford University Press, 1965.

Sunkel, Osvaldo
"Transnational Capitalism and National Disintegration in Latin America." Social and Economic Studies Journal 22:1 (March 1973): 132-176.

Sutcliffe, Bob
"Imperialism and Industrialization in the Third World." Studies in the Theory of Imperialism, pp. 171-192. Edited by Roger Owen and Bob Sutcliffe. New York: Longman, 1972.

Sweezy, P.
The Theory of Capitalist Development: Principles of Marxian Political Economy. New York: Monthly Review Press, 1972. (First published 1942).

Tanzer, Michael
The Political Economy of International Oil and the Underdeveloped Countries. Boston: Beacon Press, 1969.

United Nations. Department of Economic and Social Affairs
Multinational Corporations in World Development. New York: Praeger Publishers, 1974.

Vaupel, James W., and Curhan, Joan P.
The World's Multinational Enterprises. Boston: Harvard University Press, 1973.

IMPERIALISM (cont'd)

Veltmeyer, Henry
"Dependency and Underdevelopment: Some Questions and Problems." Canadian Journal of Political and Social Theory 2:2 (Spring 1978): 55-72.

Vernon, Raymond
Sovereignty at Bay: The Multinational Spread of U.S. Enterprises. The Harvard Multinational Enterprise series. New York: Basic Books, 1971.

Wallerstein, Immanuel
"The Rise and Future Demise of the World Capitalist System: Concepts for Comparative Analysis." Comparative Studies in Society and History 16:4 (September 1974):387-415.

The Modern World System: Capitalist Agriculture and the Origins of the European World Economy in the Sixteenth Century. New York: Academic Press, 1974.

"The Present State of the Debate on World Inequality." World Inequality: Origins and Perspectives, pp. 9-28. Edited by I. Wallerstein. Montreal: Black Rose Books, 1975.

Warren, B.
"Imperialism and Capitalist Industrialization." New Left Review 81 (September-October 1973):3-44.

Wilber, Charles K., ed.
The Political Economy of Development and Underdevelopment. New York: Random House, 1973.

Wilkins, Mira
The Emergence of Multinational Enterprise: American Business Abroad from the Colonial Era to 1914. Cambridge, Mass.: Harvard University Press, 1970.

The Maturing of Multinational Enterprise: American Business Abroad from 1914 to 1970. Cambridge, Mass.: Harvard University Press, 1974.

Wilkins, Mira, and Hill, Frank Ernest
American Business Abroad: Ford on Six Continents. Detroit: Wayne State University Press, 1964.

2. MULTINATIONALS, BRANCH PLANTS, AND CANADA

Bliss, Michael
"Canadianizing American Business: The Roots of the Branch Plant." Close the 49th Parallel Etc.: The Americanization of Canada, pp. 27-42. Edited by Ian Lumsden. Toronto: University of Toronto Press, 1970.

Calvert, J.
"The Ontario Development Corporation: The Politics of Stanley Randall." Canadian Forum 51:39 (June 1971):23-28.

Canada. Department of Trade and Commerce
Foreign Direct Investment in Canada. (The Gray Report). Ottawa: Queen's Printer, 1972.

Canada. Privy Council
Foreign Ownership and the Structure of Canadian Industry: Report of the Task Force on the Structure of Canadian Industry. (The Watkins Report). Ottawa: Queen's Printer, 1968.

Canada. Science Council
The Multinational Firm, Foreign Direct Investment and Canadian Science Policy. Special Study Number 22. Ottawa: Information Canada, 1971.

Chodos, Robert
The Caribbean Connection. A Last Post Book. Toronto: James Lorimer, 1977.

Chodos, Robert, and Burgess, Drummond
"Ma Bell Joins the Jet Set." Let Us Prey, pp. 33-49. Edited by Robert Chodos and Rae Murphy. Toronto: James Lorimer, 1974.

Clement, Wallace
"Canada and Multinational Corporations: An Overview." Modernization and the Canadian State. Edited by D. Glenday, H. Guindon, and A. Turowetz. Toronto: Macmillan (to be published 1978).

Continental Corporate Power: Economic Elite Linkages Between Canada and the United States. Toronto: McClelland and Stewart, 1977.

"The Canadian Bourgeoisie--Merely Comprador?" Imperialism, Nationalism, and Canada, pp. 71-84. Edited by John Saul and Craig Heron. Toronto: New Hogtown Press, 1977.

Davis, A.K.
"Canadian Society and History as Hinterland Versus Metropolis." Canadian Society: Pluralism, Change, and Conflict, pp. 6-32. Edited by R. Ossenberg. Scarborough: Prentice-Hall, 1971.

MULTINATIONALS, BRANCH PLANTS, AND CANADA (cont'd)

Development Education Centre, and the Latin American Working Group
"Corporate Power, the Canadian State, and Imperialism." Imperialism, Nationalism, and Canada, pp. 48-70. Edited by John Saul and Craig Heron. Toronto: New Hogtown Press, 1977.

Deverell, John, and the Latin American Working Group
Falconbridge: Portrait of a Canadian Mining Multinational. Toronto: James Lorimer, 1975.

Drache, Daniel
"What Passes for Canadian History." Canadian Dimension 8:4-5 (January 1972):38-41.

"Rediscovering Canadian Political Economy." Journal of Canadian Studies 11:3 (August 1976):3-18.

Draimin, Tim, and Swift, Jamie
"What's Canada Doing in Brazil?" This Magazine 8:5-6 (January-February 1975):3-8.

Gonick, Cy
"Foreign Ownership and Political Decay." Close the 49th Parallel Etc.: The Americanization of Canada, pp. 43-73. Edited by Ian Lumsden. Toronto: University of Toronto Press, 1969.

Grant, George
Lament for a Nation: The Defeat of Canadian Nationalism. Canada Today. Toronto: McClelland and Stewart, 1967.

Hutcheson, John
Dominance and Dependency: Liberalism and National Policies in the North Atlantic Triangle. Toronto: McClelland and Stewart, 1978.

Hymer, Stephen
"Direct Foreign Investment and the National Economic Interest." Nationalism in Canada, pp. 191-202. Edited by Peter Russell. Toronto: McGraw-Hill, 1966.

Last Post
"Brascan, Brazil and the Liberal Party." Last Post 3:2 (March 1973):28-39.

Laxer, James
"Canadian Manufacturing and U.S. Trade Policy." Canada Ltd.: The Political Economy of Dependency, pp. 127-152. Edited by Robert Laxer. Toronto: McClelland and Stewart, 1973.

MULTINATIONALS, BRANCH PLANTS AND CANADA (cont'd)

Laxer, James
"Introduction to the Political Economy of Canada." Canada Ltd.: The Political Economy of Dependency, pp. 26-41. Edited by Robert Laxer. Toronto: McClelland and Stewart, 1973.

Levitt, Kari
Silent Surrender: The Multinational Corporation in Canada. Toronto: Macmillan, 1970.

Levitt, K., and McIntyre, A.
Canada-West Indies Economic Relations. Montreal: McGill University Press, 1967.

Lewis, David
Louder Voices: The Corporate Welfare Bums. Toronto: James, Lewis and Samuel, 1972.

Litvak, I.A., and Maule, C.J.
"The Multinational Corporation: Some Perspectives." Canadian Public Administration 13:2 (Summer 1970):129-139.

Litvak, I.A.; Maule, C.J.; and Robinson, R.D.
Dual Loyalty: Canadian-U.S. Business Arrangements. Toronto: McGraw-Hill, 1971.

Mathias, Philip
Forced Growth: Five Studies of Government Involvement in the Development of Canada. Toronto: James, Lewis and Samuel, 1971.

Naylor, R.T.
"The History of Domestic and Foreign Capital in Canada." Canada Ltd.: The Political Economy of Dependency, pp. 42-56. Edited by Robert Laxer. Toronto: McClelland and Stewart, 1973.

"Dominion of Capital: Canada and International Investment." Domination, pp. 33-56. Edited by A. Kontos. Toronto: University of Toronto Press, 1975.

Neufeld, E.P.
A Global Corporation: A History of the International Development of Massey-Ferguson Limited. Toronto: University of Toronto Press, 1969.

Ontario. Task Force on Foreign Investment
Report of the Interdepartmental Task Force on Foreign Investment. Toronto: Queen's Printer, 1971.

Paquet, Gilles, ed.
The Multinational Firm and the Nation State. Don Mills, Ontario: Collier-Macmillan, 1972.

MULTINATIONALS, BRANCH PLANTS AND CANADA (cont'd)

Park, Frank, and Park, Libbie
Anatomy of Big Business. Toronto: James, Lewis and Samuel, 1973. (First published 1962).

Perry, Robert L.
Galt, U.S.A.: The "American Presence" in a Canadian City. A Financial Post Book. Toronto: Maclean-Hunter, 1971.

Pope, W.H.
The Elephant and the Mouse: A Handbook on Regaining Control of Canada's Economy. Toronto: McClelland and Stewart, 1971.

Pratt, Larry
The Tar Sands: Syncrude and the Politics of Oil. Edmonton: Hurtig Publishers, 1976.

Reuber, G.L., and Roseman, F.
The Takeover of Canadian Firms, 1945-1961. Ottawa: Queen's Printer, 1969.

Rosenbluth, G.
"The Relation Between Foreign Control and Concentration in Canadian Industry." Canadian Journal of Economics 3 (February 1970): 14-38.

Rotstein, A.
The Precarious Homestead: Essays on Economics, Technology and Nationalism. Toronto: New Press, 1973.

Rotstein, Abraham, and Lax, Gary, eds.
Independence: The Canadian Challenge. Toronto: Committee for an Independent Canada, 1972.

Safarian, A.E.
Foreign Ownership of Canadian Industry. Toronto: McGraw-Hill, 1966.

The Performance of Foreign-Owned Firms in Canada. Montreal: Canadian-American Committee, 1969.

Saul, John, and Heron, Craig, eds.
Imperialism, Nationalism and Canada. Toronto: New Hogtown Press, 1977.

Starowicz, M., and Murphy, R., eds.
Corporate Canada: 14 Probes Into the Workings of a Branch-Plant Economy. A Last Post Special. Toronto: James, Lewis and Samuel, 1972.

MULTINATIONALS, BRANCH PLANTS AND CANADA (cont'd)

Statistics Canada
Canada's International Investment Position, 1968 to 1970. Ottawa: Information Canada, 1975.

Canada's International Investment Position, 1926 to 1967. Ottawa: Information Canada, 1971.

Swift, Jamie
The Big Nickel: Inco at Home and Abroad. Kitchener: Between the Lines, 1977.

TCLPAC
"Larceny by Proxy: Gulf Oil (Canada) Ltd. and Angola." This Magazine 7:4 (January 1974):23-27.

Warnock, Jack
"Canadian Sub-Imperialism? A Reply." This Magazine 9:1 (March-April 1975):30-32.

3. CANADA-UNITED STATES RELATIONS

Aitken, Hugh G.J.
"The Changing Structure of the Canadian Economy." The American Economic Impact on Canada, pp. 3-35. Edited by H.G.J. Aitken, et al. Durham, N.C.: Duke University Press, 1959.

American Capital and Canadian Resources. Cambridge, Mass.: Harvard University Press, 1961.

Aitken, Hugh G.J., et al., eds.
The American Economic Impact on Canada. Durham, N.C.: Duke University Press, 1959.

Axline, W.A.; Hyndman, J.E.; Lyon, P; and Molot, M., eds.
Continental Community?: Independence and Integration in North America. A Carleton Contemporary. Toronto: McClelland and Stewart, 1974.

Bladen, Vincent W.
"The Size of the Establishment in Canadian and American Industry." Contributions to Canadian Economics: University of Toronto Studies, History and Economics 1 (1928):56-68.

Blyth, C.D., and Carty, E.B.
"Non-Resident Ownership of Canadian Industry." Canadian Journal of Economics and Political Science 22:4 (November 1956):449-460.

Brebner, John Bartlet
North Atlantic Triangle: The Interplay of Canada, the United States and Great Britain. The Carleton Library, no. 30. Toronto: McClelland and Stewart, 1966. (First published 1945).

Brecher, Irving
"The Flow of United States Investment Funds into Canada Since World War II." The American Economic Impact on Canada, pp. 100-126. Edited by H.G.J. Aitken, et al. Durham, N.C.: Duke University Press, 1959.

Capital Flows Between Canada and the United States. Montreal: Canadian-American Committee, 1965.

Brecher, Irving, and Reisman, S.S.
Canada-United States Economic Relations: Report of the Royal Commission on Canada's Economic Prospects. Ottawa: Queen's Printer, 1957.

Bronson, H.E.
"Continentalism and Canadian Agriculture." Capitalism and the National Question in Canada, pp. 121-140. Edited by G. Teeple. Toronto: University of Toronto Press, 1972.

CANADA-UNITED STATES RELATIONS (cont'd)

Bryce, R.B.
"The Effect on Canada of Industrial Fluctuations in the United States," Canadian Journal of Economics and Political Science 5:3 (August 1939):373-386.

Canada
Foreign Ownership and the Structure of Canadian Industry: Report of the Task Force on the Structure of Canadian Industry. (The Watkins Report). Ottawa: Queen's Printer, 1968.

Canada. Department of National Revenue
Foreign Direct Investment in Canada. (The Gray Report). Ottawa: Queen's Printer, 1965.

Canada. Royal Commission on Canada's Economic Prospects
The Gordon Commission Report. Ottawa: Queen's Printer, 1956-58.

Canada. Standing Committee on External Affairs and National Defence
Report (11th) of the Committee Respecting Canada-U.S. Relations. (The Wahn Report). Ottawa: Queen's Printer, 1970.

Canadian Forum
A Citizen's Guide to the Gray Report. Toronto: New Press, 1970.

Carr, D.W.
Recovering Canada's Nationhood. Ottawa: Canada Publishing Co., 1971.

Caves, R.E., and Holton, R.H.
The Canadian Economy, Prospect and Retrospect. Harvard Economic Studies, vol. 112. Cambridge, Mass.: Harvard University Press, 1959.

Clarkson, Stephen, ed.
An Independent Foreign Policy for Canada? A Carleton Contemporary. Toronto: McClelland and Stewart, 1968.

Clement, Wallace
Continental Corporate Power: Economic Elite Linkages Between Canada and the United States. Toronto: McClelland and Stewart, 1977.

"A Political Economy of Regionalism in Canada." Modernization and the Canadian State. Edited by D. Glenday, H. Guindon, and A. Turowetz. Toronto: Macmillan (to be published 1978).

Coats, R.H., and Maclean, M.C.
The American-Born in Canada: A Statistical Interpretation. Toronto: Ryerson Press, 1943.

Creighton, Donald G.
Canada's First Century, 1867-1967. Toronto: Macmillan, 1970.

Towards the Discovery of Canada: Selected Essays. Toronto: Macmillan, 1972.

Deutsch, John J.
"Recent American Influence in Canada, With Particular Reference to Economic Factors and Canadian Reaction." The American Economic Impact on Canada, pp. 36-50. Edited by H.G.J. Aitken, et al. Durham, N.C.: Duke University Press, 1959.

Eayrs, James
In Defence of Canada. 2 vol. Studies in the Structure of Power; Decision-Making in Canada, nos. 1 and 3. Toronto: University of Toronto Press, 1964, 1967.

Field, Frederick William
Capital Investments in Canada: Some Facts and Figures Respecting One of the Most Attractive Investment Fields in the World. Montreal: Monetary Times of Canada, 1911.

Gibson, J.D.
"The Changing Influence of the United States on the Canadian Economy." Canadian Journal of Economics and Political Science 22:4 (November 1956):421-436.

Grant, George
Lament for a Nation: The Defeat of Canadian Nationalism. Canada Today. Toronto: McClelland and Stewart, 1965.

Hillmer, N., and Stevenson, G., eds.
Foremost Nation: Canadian Foreign Policy and a Changing World. Carleton Contemporaries. Toronto: McClelland and Stewart, 1977.

Horowitz, Irving Louis
"The Hemispheric Connection: A Critique and Corrective to Entrepreneurial Thesis of Development with Special Emphasis on the Canadian Case." Queen's Quarterly 80:3 (Autumn 1973):327-359.

Howay, F.W.; Sage, W.N.; and Angus, H.F.
British Columbia and the United States: The North Pacific Slope From Fur Trade to Aviation. The Relations of Canada and the United States. Toronto: Ryerson, 1942.

Hymer, Stephen
"Direct Foreign Investment and the National Economic Interest." Nationalism in Canada, pp. 191-202. Edited by P. Russell. Toronto: McGraw-Hill, 1966.

CANADA-UNITED STATES RELATIONS (cont'd)

Innis, Harold A.
Essays in Canadian Economic History. Edited by Mary Q. Innis. Toronto: University of Toronto Press, 1956.

Johnson, Harry G.
"Canadian-American Integration in Face of a Changing World Economy." The Canadian Quandary, pp. 123-132. Toronto: McClelland and Stewart, 1977.

Kottman, Richard N.
Reciprocity and the North Atlantic Triangle, 1932-1938. Ithaca, New York: Cornell University Press, 1968.

Laxer, Robert, ed.
(Canada) Ltd.: The Political Economy of Dependency. Toronto: McClelland and Stewart, 1973.

Canada's Unions. Toronto: James Lorimer, 1976.

Levitt, Kari
Silent Surrender: The Multinational Corporation in Canada. Toronto: Macmillan, 1970.

Litvak, I., and Maule, C.J.
"Interest Group Tactics and Foreign Investment: The Time-Reader's Digest Case Study." Canadian Journal of Political Science 7:4 (December 1974):616-629.

Lumsden, Ian
"Thoughts on Canadian Dependency." This Magazine 9:5 (November-December 1975):40-45.

Lyon, P.V., and Ismael, T.Y.
Canada and the Third World. Toronto: Macmillan, 1976.

Mackintosh, W.A.
"Canadian Economic Policy from 1945 to 1957--Origins and Influences." The American Economic Impact on Canada, pp. 51-68. Edited by H.G.J. Aitken, et al. Durham, N.C.: Duke University Press, 1959.

Marshall, Herbert; Southard, Frank; and Taylor, Kenneth W.
Canadian-American Industry: A Study in International Investment. The Carleton Library, no. 93. Toronto: McClelland and Stewart, 1976. (First published 1936).

Minifie, J.M.
Peacemaker or Powdermonkey: Canada's Role in a Revolutionary World. Toronto: McClelland and Stewart, 1960.

CANADA-UNITED STATES RELATIONS (cont'd)

Pope, W.H.
The Elephant and the Mouse: A Handbook on Regaining Control of Canada's Economy. Toronto: McClelland and Stewart, 1971.

Porter, Glenn, and Cuff, Robert
Enterprise and National Development: Essays in Canadian Business and Economic History. Toronto: Hakkert, 1973.

Resnick, Philip
"Canadian Defence Policy and the American Empire." Close the 49th Parallel Etc.: The Americanization of Canada, pp. 93-115. Edited by Ian Lumsden. Toronto: University of Toronto Press, 1970.

Rosenbluth, G.
"Industrial Concentration in Canada and the United States." Canadian Journal of Economics and Political Science 20:3 (August 1954):332-346.

"The Relation Between Foreign Control and Concentration in Canadian Industry." Canadian Journal of Economics 3 (February 1970): 14-38.

Rotstein, Abraham, and Lax, Gary, eds.
Independence: The Canadian Challenge. Toronto: Committee for an Independent Canada, 1972.

Saul, J., and Heron, C., eds.
Imperialism, Nationalism and Canada. Toronto: New Hogtown Press, 1977.

Scott, J., and Howard, R.
"International Unions and the Ideology of Class Collaboration." Capitalism and the National Question in Canada, pp. 67-87. Edited by G. Teeple. Toronto: University of Toronto Press, 1972.

Stevenson, Garth
"Foreign Direct Investment and the Provinces: A Study of Elite Attitudes." Canadian Journal of Political Science 7:4 (December 1974):630-647.

"Continental Integration and National Unity." Continental Community? pp. 194-217. Edited by W. Axline, et al. Toronto: McClelland and Stewart, 1974.

Taylor, C.
Snow Job: Canada, the United States and Vietnam, 1954-73. Toronto: Anansi, 1974.

TCLSAC
"Liberals and Liberation." This Magazine 9:2 (May-June 1975):21-25.

CANADA-UNITED STATES RELATIONS (cont'd)

United States
U.S. Natural Resource Requirements and Foreign Economic Policy. Washington: International Economic Policy Association, 1974.

Viner, Jacob
Canada's Balance of International Indebtedness, 1900-1913: An Inductive Study in the Theory of International Trade. The Carleton Library, no. 86. Toronto: McClelland and Stewart, 1975. (First published 1924).

Warnock, Jack
Partner to Behemoth: The Military Policy of a Satellite Canada. Toronto: New Press, 1970.

Williams, Glen
"Canada--The Case of the Wealthiest Colony." This Magazine 10:1 (February-March 1976):28-32.

(SEE ALSO: Nationalism)

III. UNEVEN DEVELOPMENT: REGIONAL DISPARITIES

1. WEST

Avery, Donald, and Neary, Peter
"Laurier, Borden and a White British Columbia." Journal of Canadian Studies 12:4 (Summer 1977):24-34.

Badgley, Robin F., and Samuel Wolfe
Doctors' Strike: Medical Care and Conflict in Saskatchewan. Toronto: Macmillan, 1967.

Barr, John, and Anderson, Owen, eds.
The Unfinished Revolt: Some Views on Western Independence. Toronto: McClelland and Stewart, 1971.

Bercuson, D.J.
Canada and the Burden of Unity. Toronto: Macmillan, 1977.

Berger, Carl, and Cook, Ramsey, eds.
The West and the Nation: Essays in Honour of W.L. Morton. Toronto: McClelland and Stewart, 1976.

Britnell, G.E.
The Wheat Economy. Scholarly Reprint series. Toronto: University of Toronto Press, 1974. (First published 1939).

"Perspective on Change in the Prairie Economy." Canadian Journal of Economics and Political Science 19:4 (November 1953):437-454.

Brown, Lorne
"Hinterland Rebels: The Story of the Saskatchewan Farmers' Movement." Canadian Dimension 8:8 (August 1972):32-42.

Careless, J.M.S.
"Frontierism, Metropolitanism and Canadian History." Canadian Historical Review 35:1 (March 1954):1-21.

Clark, S.D.
"The Religious Sect in Canadian Economic Development." Canadian Journal of Economics and Political Science 12:4 (November 1946): 439-453.

Church and Sect in Canada. Toronto: University of Toronto Press, 1948.

"The Frontier and Democratic Theory." Proceedings and Transactions of the Royal Society of Canada 48:2 (June 1954):65-75.

WEST (cont'd)

Creighton, Donald
"Macdonald, Confederation and the West." Towards the Discovery of Canada: Selected Essays, pp. 229-242. Toronto: Macmillan, 1972.

Dafoe, John Wesley
Clifford Sifton in Relation to His Times. Toronto: Macmillan, 1931.

Dawson, Carl A.
Group Settlement: Ethnic Communities in Western Canada. Toronto: Macmillan, 1936.

Dawson, C.A., and Younge, Eva R.
Pioneering in the Prairie Provinces: The Social Side of the Settlement Process. Toronto: Macmillan, 1940.

Easterbrook, William T.
Farm Credit in Canada. Political Economy series, no. 2. Toronto: University of Toronto Press, 1938.

Fowke, Vernon
Canadian Agricultural Policy: The Historical Pattern. Toronto: University of Toronto Press, 1946.

The National Policy and the Wheat Economy. Social Credit in Alberta: Its Background and Development, no. 7. Toronto: University of Toronto Press, 1957.

Friesen, J., and Ralston, H.K., eds.
Historical Essays on British Columbia. The Carleton Library, no. 96. Toronto: McClelland and Stewart, 1976.

Gray, James H.
Winter Years: The Depression on the Prairies. Toronto: Macmillan, 1966.

Red Lights on the Prairies. Toronto: Macmillan, 1971.

Hanson, Eric
Dynamic Decade: The Evolution and Effects of the Oil Industry in Alberta. Toronto: McClelland and Stewart, 1958.

Hill, Douglas
The Opening of the Canadian West. London: Heinemann, 1967.

Horn, Michiel, ed.
The Dirty Thirties: Canadians in the Great Depression. Toronto: Copp Clark, 1972.

WEST (cont'd)

Howard, Joseph K.
Strange Empire: A Narrative of the Northwest. Toronto: James Lorimer, 1974. (First published 1952).

Knox, Paul, and Resnick, Philip, eds.
Essays in B.C. Political Economy. Vancouver: New Star Books, 1974.

Kroetsch, Robert
Alberta. The Traveller's Canada. Toronto: Macmillan, 1968.

Lipset, S.M.
Agrarian Socialism: The Cooperative Commonwealth Federation in Saskatchewan; A Study in Political Sociology. Rev. ed. Berkeley: University of California Press, 1971. (First published 1950).

MacGibbon, D.A.
The Canadian Grain Trade, 1931-1951. Toronto: University of Toronto Press, 1952. (First published 1932).

Mackintosh, W.A.
Prairie Settlement: The Geographical Setting. Canadian Frontiers of Settlement, vol. 1. Toronto: Macmillan, 1934.

"Some Aspects of a Pioneer Economy." Canadian Journal of Economics and Political Science 2:4 (November 1936):457-463.

Mallory, J.R.
Social Credit and the Federal Power in Canada. Social Credit in Alberta; Its Background and Development, no. 5. Toronto: University of Toronto Press, 1976. (First published 1954).

McCourt, Edward A.
Saskatchewan. The Traveller's Canada. Toronto: Macmillan, 1968.

Morton, Arthur S.
A History of the Canadian West to 1870-71. Toronto: Thos. Nelson and Sons, 1956.

Morton, W.L.
"The Bias of Prairie Politics." Historical Essays on the Prairie Provinces, pp. 289-300. Edited by D. Swainson. Toronto: McClelland and Stewart, 1970.

Manitoba: A History. 2nd ed. Toronto: University of Toronto Press, 1973. (First edition 1939).

"Clio in Canada: The Interpretation of Canadian History." Approaches to Canadian History, pp. 42-49. Edited by C. Berger, et al. Toronto: University of Toronto Press, 1967.

WEST (cont'd)

Ormsby, Margaret
British Columbia: A History. Toronto: Macmillan, 1958.

Paterson, D.G.; Blain, L; and Rae, J.D.
"The Regional Impact of Economic Fluctuations During the Inter-War Period: The Case of British Columbia." Canadian Journal of Economics 7:3 (August 1974):381-401.

Phillips, Paul
"National Policy, Continental Economics, and National Disintegration." Canada and the Burden of Unity, pp. 19-43. Edited by D.J. Bercuson. Toronto: Macmillan, 1977.

"The Hinterland Perspective: The Political Economy of Vernon C. Fowke." Canadian Journal of Political and Social Theory 2:2 (Spring 1978):73-96.

Porritt, Edward
The Revolt in Canada Against the New Feudalism. London: Cassell and Co., 1911.

Pratt, Larry
"The State and Province-Building: Alberta's Development Strategy." The Canadian State: Political Economy and Political Power, pp. 133-162. Edited by Leo Panitch. Toronto: University of Toronto Press, 1977.

Pratt, Larry, and Richards, John
The New West. Toronto: McClelland and Stewart (forthcoming).

Regehr, T.D.
"Western Canada and the Burden of National Transportation Policies." Canada and the Burden of Unity, pp. 115-141. Edited by D.J. Bercuson. Toronto: Macmillan, 1977.

Rich, Edwin E.
The History of the Hudson's Bay Company, 1670-1870. 3 vol. Toronto: McClelland and Stewart, 1960, 1961.

Robin, Martin
The Rush for Spoils: The Company Province, 1871-1933. Toronto: McClelland and Stewart, 1972.

Smith, David E.
"Western Politics and National Unity." Canada and the Burden of Unity, pp. 142-168. Edited by D.J. Bercuson. Toronto: Macmillan, 1977.

WEST (cont'd)

Stanley, G.F.
The Birth of Western Canada: A History of the Riel Rebellions. Toronto: University of Toronto Press, 1961.

Swainson, Donald, ed.
Historical Essays on the Prairie Provinces. The Carleton Library, no. 53. Toronto: McClelland and Stewart, 1970.

Thompson, John Herd
The Harvests of War: The Prairie West, 1914-1918. Toronto: McClelland and Stewart, 1978.

Usher, Peter
"Hinterland Culture Shock." Canadian Dimension 8:8 (August 1972): 22-29.

Woodcock, George
Gabriel Dumont: The Métis Chief and His Lost World. Edmonton: Hurtig Publishers, 1975.

Young, Walter D.
Democracy and Discontent: Progressivism, Socialism and Social Credit in the Canadian West. The Frontenac Library, no. 2. Toronto: Ryerson Press, 1969.

(SEE ALSO: National Policy, Resources, AND Political Parties)

2. ATLANTIC

Acheson, T.W.

The Social Origins of Canadian Industrialization: A Study in the Structure of Entrepreneurship. (Unpublished PhD. Thesis). University of Toronto, 1972.

"The Maritimes and 'Empire Canada'." Canada and the Burden of Unity, pp. 87-114. Edited by D.J. Bercuson. Toronto: Macmillan, 1977.

Alexander, David

"Development and Dependence in Newfoundland 1880-1970." Acadiensis 4:1 (Autumn 1974):3-31.

"The Collapse of the Saltfish Trade and Newfoundland's Integration into the North American Economy." Canadian Historical Association Historical Papers (1976):229-248.

"Newfoundland's Traditional Economy and Development to 1934." Acadiensis 5:2 (Spring 1976):56-78.

"The Political Economy of Fishing in Newfoundland." Journal of Canadian Studies 11:1 (February 1976):32-40.

Archibald, Bruce

"Atlantic Regional Underdevelopment and Socialism." Essays on the Left: Essays in Honour of T.C. Douglas, pp. 103-120. Edited by Laurier Lapierre, et al. Toronto: McClelland and Stewart, 1971.

Atlantic Development Council

A Strategy for the Economic Development of the Atlantic Region, 1971-1981. Fredericton, N.B.: Queen's Printer, 1971.

Atlantic Provinces Economic Council

The Atlantic Provinces in Relation to the Canadian Economy, 1867-1955. Moncton: Queen's Printer, 1955.

Royal Commission Reports and Related Action: A Review of Recommendations and Policy on Economic Issues in the Maritime Provinces, 1926-1960. Halifax: Queen's Printer, 1969.

Sixth Annual Review: The Atlantic Economy. Halifax: Queen's Printer, 1972.

Bailey, A.G.

"Railways and the Confederation Issue in New Brunswick, 1863-1865." Culture and Nationality, pp. 76-92. The Carleton Library, no. 58. Toronto: McClelland and Stewart, 1972.

ATLANTIC (cont'd)

Bailey, A.G.
"The Basis and Persistence of Opposition to Confederation in New Brunswick." Culture and Nationality, pp. 93-117. The Carleton Library, no. 58. Toronto: McClelland and Stewart, 1972.

"New Brunswick: Keystone of the Arch." Culture and Nationality, pp. 118-127. The Carleton Library, no. 58. Toronto: McClelland and Stewart, 1972.

"Creative Moments in the Culture of the Maritime Provinces." Culture and Nationality, pp. 44-57. The Carleton Library, no. 58. Toronto: McClelland and Stewart, 1972.

Beck, J. Murray, ed.
Joseph Howe: Voice of Nova Scotia; A Selection. The Carleton Library, no. 20. Toronto: McClelland and Stewart, 1964.

Brebner, John Bartlet
New England's Outpost: Acadia Before the Conquest of Canada. Studies in History, Economics and Public Law, no. 293. New York: Columbia University Press, 1927.

The Neutral Yankees of Nova Scotia: A Marginal Colony During the Revolutionary Years. The Carleton Library, no. 45. Toronto: McClelland and Stewart, 1969.

Brookes, Alan
"Out-migration from the Maritime Provinces, 1860-1900: Some Preliminary Considerations." Acadiensis 5:2 (Spring 1976):26-55.

Brown, Cassie
Death on the Ice: The Great Newfoundland Sealing Disaster of 1914. Toronto: Doubleday, 1974.

Brox, Ottar
Maintenance of Economic Dualism in Newfoundland. Newfoundland Social and Economic Studies, no. 9. St. John's: Institute of Social and Economic Research, Memorial University of Newfoundland, 1969.

Cameron, James Malcolm
Industrial History of the New Glasgow District. New Glasgow, N.S.: Hector Publishing Company, 1960.

The Pictonian Colliers. Halifax: Nova Scotia Museum, 1974.

Cameron, Silver Donald
The Education of Everett Richardson: The Nova Scotia Fishermen's Strike, 1970-71. Toronto: McClelland and Stewart, 1977.

ATLANTIC (cont'd)

Canada. Dominion Bureau of Statistics
The Maritime Provinces in Their Relation to the National Economy of Canada: A Statistical Study of Their Social and Economic Condition. Ottawa: Queen's Printer, 1948.

Canada. Dominion Bureau of Statistics
Maritime Provinces Since Confederation: A Statistical Study of Their Social and Economic Condition During the Past Sixty Years. Ottawa: Queen's Printer, 1927.

Canada. Dominion Bureau of Statistics
Report of the Royal Commission on Maritime Claims. Ottawa: Queen's Printer, 1926.

Canada. Economic Council
Living Together: A Study of Regional Disparities. Ottawa: Ministry of Supply and Services, 1977.

Canada. Economic Council
Second Annual Review. Ottawa: Queen's Printer, 1965.

Canada. Royal Commission on Coal
Report, 1946. Ottawa: Queen's Printer, 1947.

Careless, J.M.S.
"Aspects of Metropolitanism in Atlantic Canada." Regionalism in the Canadian Community, 1867-1967, pp. 117-129. Edited by Mason Wade. Toronto: University of Toronto Press, 1969.

Cayley, David
"Underdeveloping Prince Edward Island: The P.E.I. 'Development Plan'." This Magazine 8:3 (August-September 1974):3-7.

Clairmont, Donald H., and Magill, Dennis W.
Africville: The Life and Death of a Canadian Black Community. Toronto: McClelland and Stewart, 1974.

Clark, A.H.
"Contributions of Its Southern Neighbours to the Development of the Maritime Provinces Area, 1710-1867." The Influence of the United States on Canadian Development: Eleven Case Studies, pp. 164. Edited by Richard Preston. Durham, N.C.: Duke University Press, 1972.

Acadia: The Geography of Early Nova Scotia to 1769. Madison, Wisc.: University of Wisconsin Press, 1968.

Cullen, M.K.
"The Transportation Issue, 1873-1973." Canada's Smallest Province: A History of P.E.I., pp. 232-263. Edited by F.W.P. Bolger. Charlottetown: Prince Edward Island 1973 Centennial Commission, 1973.

ATLANTIC (cont'd)

Currie, A.W.
"The Maritime Freight Rates Act." Canadian Transportation Economics, pp. 113-121. By A. Currie. Toronto: University of Toronto Press, 1967.

Fay, C.R.
Life and Labour in Newfoundland. Toronto: University of Toronto Press, 1956.

"Problems of Maritime Provinces." Dalhousie Review 4:4 (January 1925):438-451.

Fay, C.R., and Innis, H.A.
"The Economic Development of Canada, 1867-1921: The Maritime Provinces." The Cambridge History of the British Empire, vol. 6, pp. 657-671. Edited by J. Holland Rose, et al. Cambridge: Cambridge University Press, 1930.

Fergusson, C.B.
The Labour Movement in Nova Scotia Before Confederation. Halifax: Public Archives of Nova Scotia, 1964.

Fingard, Judith
"The Winter's Tale: The Seasonal Contours of Pre-industrial Poverty in British America, 1815-1860." Canadian Historical Association Historical Papers (1974):65-94.

Forbes, E.R.
"The Origins of the Maritime Rights Movement." Acadiensis 5:1 (Autumn 1975):56-66.

"Misguided Symmetry: The Destruction of Regional Transportation Policy for the Maritimes." Canada and the Burden of Unity, pp. 60-86. Edited by D.J. Bercuson. Toronto: Macmillan, 1977.

Forsey, Eugene
National Problems of Canada: Economic and Social Aspects of the Nova Scotia Coal Industry. McGill University Economic Studies, no. 5. Toronto: Macmillan, 1926.

"Some Notes on the Early History of Unions in P.E.I." Canadian Historical Review 46:4 (December 1965):346-351.

Frank, David
"Class Conflict in the Coal Industry: Cape Breton 1922." Essays in Canadian Working Class History, pp. 161-184. Edited by Gregory S. Kealey and Peter Warrian. Toronto: McClelland and Stewart, 1976.

Fraser, Dawn
Echoes From Labour's War: Industrial Cape Breton in the 1920's. Toronto: New Hogtown Press, 1976.

ATLANTIC (cont'd)

Fredericks, Hal, and Chambers, Allan
Bricklin. Fredericton: Brunswick Press, 1977.

George, Roy E.
A Leader and a Laggard: Manufacturing Industry in Nova Scotia, Quebec, and Ontario. Atlantic Provinces Studies, no. 2. Toronto: University of Toronto Press, 1970.

Grant, Ruth Fulton
The Canadian Atlantic Fishery. Toronto: Ryerson Press, 1934.

Great Britain, Government of
Newfoundland Royal Commission 1933: Report. (The Amulree Report). London: Queen's Printer, 1933.

Gwyn, Richard J.
Smallwood: The Unlikely Revolutionary. Rev. ed. Toronto: McClelland and Stewart, 1972.

Henry, Frances
The Forgotten Canadians: The Blacks of Nova Scotia. Canadian Social Problems series. Don Mills, Ont.: Longmans, 1973.

Hunt, Russell, and Campbell, Robert
K.C. Irving: The Art of the Industrialist. Toronto: McClelland and Stewart, 1973.

Innis, Harold Adams
The Cod Fisheries: The History of an International Economy. Newfoundland Social and Economic Studies, no. 6. Rev. ed. Toronto: University of Toronto Press, 1954. (First edition 1940).

Iverson, Noel, and Matthews, D. Ralph
Communities in Decline: An Examination of Household Resettlement in Newfoundland. Newfoundland Social and Economic Studies, no. 6. St. John's: Institute of Social and Economic Research, Memorial University of Newfoundland, 1968.

Kierstead, B.S.
The Economic Effects of the War on the Maritime Provinces of Canada. Halifax: Institute of Public Affairs, Dalhousie University, 1944.

Laidlaw, Alexander F., ed.
The Man From Margaree: Writings and Speeches of M.M. Coady. Toronto: McClelland and Stewart, 1971.

Levitt, Kari
Population Movements in the Atlantic Provinces. Halifax: Atlantic Provinces Economic Council, 1960.

ATLANTIC (cont'd)

Levy, Thomas A.
"The International Economic Interests and Activities of the Atlantic Provinces." American Review of Canadian Studies 5:1 (Spring 1975):98-113.

MacEwan, Paul
Miners and Steelworkers: Labour Unions in Cape Breton. Toronto: Hakkert, 1975.

Macgillivray, Don
"Cape Breton in the 1920's: A Community Besieged." Essays in Cape Breton History, pp. 49-67. Edited by B. Tennyson. Windsor, N.S.: Lancelot Press, 1973.

"Military Aid to the Civil Power: The Cape Breton Experience in the 1920's." Acadiensis 3:2 (Spring 1974):45-65.

MacPherson, Ian
"Patterns in the Maritime Co-operative Movement 1900-1945." Acadiensis 5:1 (Autumn 1975):67-83.

Mannion, John
Irish Settlements in Eastern Canada: A Study of Cultural Transfer and Adaptation. Dept. of Geography Research Publications, no. 12. Toronto: University of Toronto Press, 1974.

Mathias, Philip
Forced Growth: Five Studies of Government Involvement in the Development of Canada. Toronto: James, Lewis and Samuel, 1971.

Matthews, Ralph
"Perspectives on Recent Newfoundland Politics." Journal of Canadian Studies 9:2 (May 1974):20-35.

"There's No Better Place Than Here": Social Change in Three Newfoundland Communities. Toronto: Peter Martin Associates, 1976.

McCutcheon, Sean
Resources and Development in Newfoundland. St. John's: Development Education Centre, 1975.

McDonald, D.J.
Population Migration and Economic Development in the Atlantic Provinces. Research paper, no. 6. Fredericton: Research Centre, Atlantic Provinces Economic Council, 1968.

Muise, D.A.
"The Federal Election of 1867 in Nova Scotia: An Economic Interpretation." Collections of the Nova Scotia Historical Society 36 (1968):327-351.

ATLANTIC (cont'd)

Muise, D.A.
"Parties and Constituencies: Federal Elections in Nova Scotia, 1867-1896." Canadian Historical Association Historical Papers (1971):183-202.

Neary, Peter
"'Traditional' and 'Modern' Elements in the Social and Economic History of Bell Island and Conception Bay." Canadian Historical Association Historical Papers (1973):105-136.

"Bell Island: A Newfoundland Mining Community, 1896-1966." Canada's Visual History, Series 1 (slides).

Neary, Peter, ed.
The Political Economy of Newfoundland 1929-1972. Issues in Canadian History. Toronto: Copp Clark, 1973.

Neill, R.F.
"National Policy and Regional Development: A Footnote to the Deutsch Report on Maritime Union." Journal of Canadian Studies 9:2 (May 1974):12-20.

New Brunswick
Report of New Brunswick Committee on Reconstruction. 2 vols. Fredericton: King's Printer, 1944.

Noel, S.J.R.
Politics in Newfoundland. Toronto: University of Toronto Press, 1971.

Nova Scotia. Royal Commission on Provincial Development and Rehabilitation
Report. 2 vols. Halifax: King's Printer, 1944.

Nova Scotia. Royal Commission on Provincial Economic Inquiry
Report. Halifax: King's Printer, 1934.

Opportunities for Youth
The People's History of Cape Breton. Halifax: Opportunities for Youth, 1971.

Panting, G.E.
"The Fishermen's Protective Union of Newfoundland and the Farmers' Organizations in Western Canada." Canadian Historical Association Report (1963):141-151.

Prowse, D.W.
A History of Newfoundland, from the English, Colonial, and Foreign Records. 3rd. ed. St. John's, Nfld.: Dicks, 1971. (First published 1895).

ATLANTIC (cont'd)

Pryke, Ken
"The Making of a Province: Nova Scotia and Confederation." Canadian Historical Association Historical Papers (1968):35-48.

"Labour and Politics: Nova Scotia at Confederation." Social History 6 (November 1970):33-55.

Rawlyk, G.A., ed.
Historical Essays on the Atlantic Provinces. The Carleton Library, no. 35. Toronto: McClelland and Stewart, 1967.

"The Farmer-Labour Movement and the Failure of Socialism in Nova Scotia." Essays on the Left, pp. 3-41. Edited by L. Lapierre, et al. Toronto: McClelland and Stewart, 1971.

"The Maritimes and the Canadian Community." Regionalism in the Canadian Community, 1867-1967, pp. 100-116. Edited by Mason Wade. Toronto: University of Toronto Press, 1969.

Saunders, S.A.
The Economic Welfare of the Maritime Provinces. Economic Publications, no. 1. Wolfville, N.S.: Acadia University, 1932.

Studies in the Economy of the Maritime Provinces. Studies of the Institute of Public Affairs at Dalhousie University. Toronto: Macmillan, 1939.

The Economic History of the Maritime Provinces. A Study Prepared for the Royal Commission on Dominion-Provincial Relations. Ottawa: King's Printer, 1939.

Sharpe, Errol
A People's History of Prince Edward Island. Toronto: Steel Rail Press, 1976.

Smallwood, Joseph Robert
Coaker of Newfoundland: The Man Who Led the Deep-Sea Fishermen to Political Power. London: Labour Publishing, 1927.

The Book of Newfoundland. 6 vols. St. John's: Newfoundland Book Publishers Ltd., 1937, 1967, 1976.

I Chose Canada: The Memoirs of the Hon. Joseph R. ("Joey") Smallwood. Toronto: Macmillan, 1973.

Smith, Philip
Brinco: The Story of Churchill Falls. Toronto: McClelland and Stewart, 1976.

ATLANTIC (cont'd)

Wadel, Cato
Now Whose Fault Is That? The Struggle for Self Esteem in the Face of Chronic Unemployment. Newfoundland Social and Economic Studies, no. 11. St. John's: Institute of Social and Economic Research, Memorial University of Newfoundland, 1973.

Wilbur, Richard
"Maritimes: Planned Underdevelopment." Canadian Dimension 7:7 (January-February 1971):14-18.

Woodfine, W.J.
"Canada's Atlantic Provinces: A Study in Regional Economic Retardation." Economics Canada: Recent Readings, pp. 312-319. Edited by D. Forster and M. Watkins. Toronto: McGraw-Hill, 1963.

3. NORTH

Berger, Thomas
Northern Frontier, Northern Homeland: The Report of the Mackenzie Valley Pipeline Inquiry. Ottawa: Supply and Services Canada, 1977.

Brody, Hugh
The People's Land: Eskimos and Whites in the Eastern Arctic. Harmondsworth: Penguin, 1975.

Canada. Science Council. Committee on Northern Development
Discussion Paper on Northern Development. Ottawa: Information Canada, 1975.

Canadian Forum
(Special Issue on the North). 55:666 (November 1976).

Chamberlin, J.E.
The Harrowing of Eden: White Attitudes Toward North American Natives. Toronto: Fitzhenry and Whiteside, 1975.

Crowe, Keith J.
A History of the Original Peoples of Northern Canada. Montreal: McGill-Queen's University Press, 1974.

Davis, R., and Zannis, M.
The Genocide Machine in Canada: The Pacification of the North. Montreal: Black Rose Books, 1973.

Dosman, Edgar J.
The National Interest: The Politics of Northern Development 1968-75. Canada in Transition. Toronto: McClelland and Stewart, 1975.

Elias, P.D.
Metropolis and Hinterland in Northern Manitoba. Winnipeg: Manitoba Museum, 1975.

Fumoleau, René
As Long as This Land Shall Last: A History of Treaty 9 and Treaty 11, 1870-1939. Toronto: McClelland and Stewart, 1973.

Gauvin, W.H., et al.
"Northern Development: A Paper for Discussion." Issues in Canadian Science Policy 3 (June 1976).

Keith, Robert F., et al.
Northern Development and Technology Assessment Systems. Ottawa:Science Council of Canada, Background Study Number 34, January 1976.

NORTH (cont'd)

Lotz, Jim
Northern Realities: The Future of Northern Development in Canada. Toronto: New Press, 1970.

Macdonald, R., ed.
The Arctic Frontier. Toronto: University of Toronto Press, 1966.

McCullum, Hugh, and McCullum, Karmel
This Land is Not For Sale. Toronto: Anglican Book Centre, 1975.

McCullum, Hugh; McCullum, Karmel; and Olthius, John
Moratorium: Justice, Energy, North and the Native People. Toronto: Anglican Book Centre, 1977.

Mowat, Farley
Canada North Now: The Great Betrayal. Toronto: McClelland and Stewart, 1976.

O'Malley, Martin
The Past and Future Land: An Account of the Berger Inquiry Into the Mackenzie Valley Pipeline. Toronto: Peter Martin Associates, 1976.

Pearse, Peter H., ed.
The Mackenzie Pipeline: Arctic Gas and Canadian Energy Policy. Toronto: McClelland and Stewart, 1974.

Phillips, R.A.J.
Canada's North. Toronto: Macmillan, 1967.

Pimlott, D.H.
Oil Under the Ice. Ottawa: Canadian Arctic Resources Committee, 1976.

Pimlott, D.H., et al.
Arctic Alternatives. Ottawa: Canadian Arctic Resources Committee, 1973.

Rea, K.J.
The Political Economy of the Canadian North: An Interpretation of the Course of Development in the Northern Territories of Canada to the Early 1960s. Toronto: University of Toronto Press, 1968.

The Political Economy of Northern Development. Background Study Number 36. Ottawa: Science Council of Canada, April 1976.

Richardson, Boyce
Strangers Devour the Land. Toronto: Macmillan, 1976.

NORTH (cont'd)

Rohmer, Richard
The Arctic Imperative: An Overview of the Energy Crisis. Toronto: McClelland and Stewart, 1973.

Surette, Ralph; Davis, Bob; and Zannis, Mark
"The International Wolf Pack Moves in on the North." Last Post 3:3 (May 1973):24-30.

Usher, Peter
The Bankslanders: Economy and Ecology of a Frontier and Trapping Community. 3 vols. Ottawa: Information Canada, 1970.

Watkins, Mel
"The Berger Report (or: The Energy Trade in Canada)." This Magazine 11:4 (July-August 1977):4-7.

Watkins, Mel, ed.
Dene Nation: The Colony Within. Toronto: University of Toronto Press, 1977.

Wonders, William C., ed.
Canada's Changing North. The Carleton Library, no. 55. Toronto: McClelland and Stewart, 1971.

Woodford, James
The Violated Vision: The Rape of Canada's North. Toronto: McClelland and Stewart, 1972.

Zaslow, Morris
The Opening of the Canadian North, 1870-1914. Toronto: McClelland and Stewart, 1971.

IV. CLASS FORMATIONS

1. CAPITALIST CLASS

Acheson, T.W.
"The Social Origins of the Canadian Industrial Elite, 1880-1885." Canadian Business History, Selected Studies, 1497-1971, pp. 144-174. Edited by D.S. Macmillan. Toronto: McClelland and Stewart, 1972.

"Changing Social Origins of the Canadian Industrial Elite, 1880-1910." Business History Review 47:2 (Summer 1973):189-217.

Aitken, H.G.J.
"Government and Business in Canada: An Interpretation." Business History Review 38:1 (Spring 1964):4-21.

Bliss, Michael
"'Dyspepsia of the Mind': The Canadian Businessman and His Enemies, 1880-1914." Canadian Business History, Selected Studies, 1497-1971, pp. 175-191. Edited by D.S. Macmillan. Toronto: McClelland and Stewart, 1972.

A Living Profit: Studies in the Social History of Canadian Business, 1883-1911. Canadian Social History. Toronto: McClelland and Stewart, 1974.

Burton, C.L.
A Sense of Urgency: Memoirs of a Canadian Merchant. Toronto: Clarke Irwin, 1952.

Chodos, R., and Murphy, R., eds.
Let Us Prey. Toronto: James Lorimer, 1974.

Clark, S.D.
The Developing Canadian Community. Toronto: University of Toronto Press, 1962.

Clement, Wallace
"Inside 'The Canadian Establishment': Trivia or Tempest?" This Magazine 10:2 (April-May 1976):30-32.

"The Changing Structure of the Canadian Economy." Canadian Review of Sociology and Anthropology (Special Summer Issue 1974): 3-27.

"Inequality of Access: Characteristics of the Canadian Corporate Elite." Canadian Review of Sociology and Anthropology 12:1 (February 1975):33-52.

CAPITALIST CLASS (cont'd)

Clement, Wallace
The Canadian Corporate Elite: An Analysis of Economic Power. The Carleton Library, no. 89. Toronto: McClelland and Stewart, 1975.

"The Corporate Elite, the Capitalist Class and the Canadian State." The Canadian State: Political Economy and Political Power, pp. 225-248. Edited by Leo Panitch. Toronto: University of Toronto Press, 1977.

Continental Corporate Power: Economic Elite Linkages Between Canada and the United States. Toronto: McClelland and Stewart, 1977.

Creighton, Donald G.
The Empire of the St. Lawrence. Toronto: Macmillan, 1956. (First published 1937).

"The Decline and Fall of the Empire of the St. Lawrence." Canadian Historical Association Historical Papers (1969):14-25.

"The Commercial Class in Canadian Politics, 1792-1840." Towards the Discovery of Canada: Selected Essays, pp. 84-102. Toronto: Macmillan, 1972.

Cuneo, Carl
"The Controlled Entry of Canadian Managers to the United States." International Journal of Comparative Sociology 18:1-2 (March-June 1977):81-101.

Davis, Robert; Zannis, Mark; and Surette, Ralph
"Why David Rockefeller was in Quebec City." Let Us Prey, pp. 94-107. Edited by Robert Chodos and Rae Murphy. Toronto: James Lorimer, 1974.

Deaton, Rick
"The Fiscal Crisis of the State and the Revolt of the Public Employee." Our Generation 8:4 (October 1972):11-51.

Drache, Daniel
"The Canadian Bourgeoisie and Its National Consciousness." Close the 49th Parallel Etc.: The Americanization of Canada, pp. 3-25. Edited by Ian Lumsden. Toronto: University of Toronto Press, 1970.

Goodwin, Crawford D.W.
Canadian Economic Thought: The Political Economy of a Developing Nation, 1814-1914. Commonwealth Studies Centre, publication no. 15. Durham, N.C.: Duke University Press, 1961.

CAPITALIST CLASS (cont'd)

Katz, Michael B.
"The Entrepreneurial Class in a Canadian City: The Mid-Nineteenth Century." Journal of Social History 8:2 (Winter 1975):1-29.

Macpherson, Mary-Etta
Shopkeepers to a Nation: The Eatons. Toronto: McClelland and Stewart, 1963.

McDougall, W.J., and Fogelbert, G.
Corporate Boards in Canada: How 64 Directorates Function. The School of Business Administration Research series. London, Ont.: University of Western Ontario, 1968.

Myers, G.
A History of Canadian Wealth. 1st Canadian ed. Toronto: James, Lewis and Samuel, 1972. (First published 1914).

Naylor, R.T.
"Dominion of Capital: Canada and International Investment." Domination, pp. 33-56. Edited by A. Kontos. Toronto: University of Toronto Press, 1975.

The History of Canadian Business, 1867-1914. 2 vols. Toronto: James Lorimer, 1975.

"Rise and Fall of the Third Commercial Empire of the St. Lawrence." Capitalism and the National Question in Canada, pp. 1-41. Edited by G. Teeple. Toronto: University of Toronto Press, 1972.

Newman, Peter
The Canadian Establishment. 2 vols. Toronto: McClelland and Stewart, 1975, 1978.

Niosi, Jorge
"La nouvelle bourgeoisie canadienne-française." Les Cahiers du Socialisme 1 (Printemps 1978):5-50.

Parai, Louis
Immigration and Emigration of Professional and Skilled Manpower During the Post-War Period. Economic Council of Canada Special Study, no. 1. Ottawa: Queen's Printer, 1965.

Park, Frank, and Park, Libbie
Anatomy of Big Business. Toronto: James, Lewis and Samuel, 1973. (First published 1962).

Piédalue, Gilles
"Les groupes financiers et la guerre du papier au Canada 1920-1930." Revue d'histoire de l'Amérique française 30:2 (September 1976):223-258.

CAPITALIST CLASS (cont'd)

Porter, Glen, and Cuff, Robert, eds.
Enterprise and National Development: Essays in Canadian Business and Economic History. Toronto: Hakkert, 1973.

Porter, John
The Vertical Mosaic: An Analysis of Social Class and Power in Canada. Studies in the Structure of Power: Decision-Making in Canada, no. 2. Toronto: University of Toronto Press, 1965.

Roussopoulos, D., ed.
The Political Economy of the State: Quebec, Canada, U.S.A. Montreal: Black Rose Books, 1973.

Starowicz, Mark, and Murphy, Rae, eds.
Corporate Canada: 14 Probes Into the Workings of a Branch-Plant Economy. A Last Post Special. Toronto: James, Lewis and Samuel, 1972.

Tulchinsky, Gerald J.J.
"The Montreal Business Community, 1837-1853." Canadian Business History: Selected Studies, 1497-1971, pp. 125-143. Edited by D.S. Macmillan. Toronto: McClelland and Stewart, 1972.

The River Barons. Toronto: University of Toronto Press, 1976.

Wilson, Alan
John Northway: A Blue Serge Canadian. Toronto: Burns and MacEachern, 1965.

Wise, S.F.
"Upper Canada and the Conservative Tradition." Profiles of a Province: Studies in the History of Ontario, pp. 20-33. Toronto: Ontario Historical Society, 1967.

Young, Bert
"Corporate Interests and the State: Anti-Combine Activity in Canada--1900 to 1970." Our Generation 10:1 (Winter/Spring 1974): 70-83.

2. CLASS CONFLICT

Abella, I.M.

"Lament for a Union Movement." Close the 49th Parallel, Etc.: The Americanization of Canada, pp. 75-91. Edited by Ian Lumsden. Toronto: University of Toronto Press, 1970.

Nationalism, Communism and Canadian Labour: The CIO, the Communist Party, and the Canadian Congress of Labour, 1935-1956. Toronto: University of Toronto Press, 1973.

Abella, I.M., ed.

On Strike: Six Key Labour Struggles in Canada, 1919-1949. Major Strikes in Canadian History. Toronto: James Lorimer, 1975.

Adams, Ian

The Poverty Wall. Toronto: McClelland and Stewart, 1970.

The Real Poverty Report. Edmonton: M.G. Hurtig, 1971.

Ames, H.B.

The City Below the Hill: A Sociological Study of a Portion of of the City of Montreal, Canada. The Social History of Canada. Toronto: University of Toronto Press, 1972. (First published 1897).

Archibald, Peter

Social Psychology as Political Economy. Toronto: McGraw-Hill Ryerson, 1978.

Avery, Donald

"Canadian Immigration Policy and the 'Foreign' Navvy, 1896-1914." Canadian Historical Association Historical Papers (1972):135-156.

"Continental European Immigrant Workers in Canada, 1896-1919: From 'Stalwart Peasants' to Radical Proletariat." Canadian Review of Sociology and Anthropology 12:1 (February 1975):53-64.

"Immigration to Western Canada, 1896-1914." Canada's Visual History, Series 1 (slides).

Babcock, Robert

Gompers in Canada: A Study in American Continentalism Before the First World War. Toronto: University of Toronto Press, 1974.

"Sam Gompers and the Expansion of the AF of L into Canada, 1882-98." Relations Industrielles/Industrial Relations 27 (August 1972).

"Samuel Gompers and the Berlin Decisions of 1902." The Influence of the United States on Canadian Development: Eleven Case Studies, pp. 185-204. Edited by R.A. Preston. Durham, N.C.: Duke University Press, 1972.

CLASS CONFLICT (cont'd)

Baird, Irene
Waste Heritage. Laurentian Library, no. 18. Toronto: Macmillan, 1973. (First published 1939).

Beckow, S.M.
"Keeping British Columbia White: Anti-Orientalism in the Canadian West, 1874-1905." Canada's Visual History, Series 1 (slides).

Bélanger, Noël, et al.
Les travailleurs québécois, 1851-1896. Collection Histoire des travailleurs québécois, 2. Montréal: Les Presses de l'Université du Québec, 1973.

Bercuson, David J.
Confrontation at Winnipeg: Labour, Industrial Relations and the General Strike. Montreal: McGill-Queen's University Press, 1974.

"1919: A Year of Strikes." Canada's Visual History, Series 1 (slides).

Fools and Wise Men: The Rise and Fall of the One Big Union. Toronto: McGraw-Hill Ryerson, 1978.

Birney, Earle
Down the Long Table. New Canadian Library, no. 117. Toronto: McClelland and Stewart, 1975. (First published 1955).

Bourque, Gilles
Question nationale et classés sociales au Québec (1760-1840). Collection Aspects, 7. Montréal: Editions Parti Pris, 1970.

Bourque, G., and Frenette, L.
"Social Classes and Nationalist Ideologies in Quebec, 1760-1970." Capitalism and the National Question in Canada, pp. 185-210. Edited by G. Teeple. Toronto: University of Toronto Press, 1972.

Bradwin, Edmund W.
The Bunkhouse Man: A Study of Work and Pay in the Camps of Canada, 1903-1914. The Social History of Canada. Toronto: University of Toronto Press, 1972. (First published 1928).

Brennan, Terence
"Lumbering in the Ottawa Valley." Canada's Visual History, Series 1 (slides).

Broadfoot, Barry
Ten Lost Years, 1929-1939: Memories of Canadians Who Survived the Depression. Toronto: Doubleday, 1973.

Brodie, Steve
Bloody Sunday, Vancouver 1938. Vancouver: Young Communist League, 1974.

Brown, Lorne
"Peace and Harmony: Breaking Down Myths of Canadian Labour History." Canadian Dimension 9:5 (May 1973):11-35.

Buchbinder, Howard
"Guaranteed Annual Income." Canadian Dimension 7:4 (October-November 1969).

Buck, Tim
Our Fight for Canada: Selected Writings (1923-1959). Toronto: Progress Books, 1959.

Canada: The Communist Viewpoint. Toronto: Progress Books, 1948.

Steps to Power: A Program of Action for the Trade Union Minority of Canada. Toronto: Trade Union Educational League, 1925.

Cameron, Silver Donald
The Education of Everett Richardson: The Nova Scotia Fishermen's Strike, 1970-71. Toronto: McClelland and Stewart, 1977.

Campbell, Ken
"Class Analysis and Technological Determinism." Alternate Routes 1 (1977):131-141.

Canada
Canada Investigates Industrialism: Royal Commission on the Relations of Labour and Capital 1889. The Social History of Canada. Edited by Greg Kealey. Toronto: University of Toronto Press, 1973.

Canada
The White Paper on Employment and Income. Ottawa: King's Printer, 1945.

Canada. Council on Social Development
Guaranteed Annual Income: An Integrated Approach. Ottawa: Runge Press, 1972.

Canada. Special Senate Committee on Poverty
Poverty in Canada. Ottawa: Information Canada, 1971.

Carter, Dyson
Fatherless Sons. Toronto: Progress Books, 1955.

CLASS CONFLICT (cont'd)

Copp, Terry
"Poverty in Montreal 1897-1921." Canada's Visual History, Series 1 (slides).

The Anatomy of Poverty: The Condition of the Working Class in Montreal, 1897-1929. The Canadian Social History series. Toronto: McClelland and Stewart, 1974.

Crispo, John
International Unionism: A Study in Canadian-American Relations. Toronto: McGraw-Hill, 1967.

Cross, Michael
"Stony Monday, 1849: The Rebellion Losses Riots in Bytown." Ontario History 63 (September 1971):177.

"The Shiners' War: Social Violence in the Ottawa Valley in the 1930s." Canadian Historical Review 54:1 (March 1973):1-26.

The Workingman in the Nineteenth Century. Toronto: Oxford University Press, 1974.

Drache, Daniel, ed.
Quebec--Only the Beginning: The Manifestoes of the Common Front. Studies Quebec, 1. Toronto: New Press, 1972.

Dumas, Evelyn
The Bitter Thirties in Quebec. Montreal: Black Rose Books, 1975.

Duncan, Kenneth
"Irish Famine Immigration and the Social Structure of Canada West." Studies in Canadian Social History, pp. 140-163. Edited by Michiel Horn and Ronald Sabourin. Toronto: McClelland and Stewart, 1974. Reprinted from Canadian Review of Sociology and Anthropology 2:1 (February 1965):19-40.

Fergusson, C.B.
The Labour Movement in Nova Scotia Before Confederation. Bulletin, no. 20. Halifax: Public Archives of Nova Scotia, 1964.

Ferns, Henry, and Ostry, Bernard
The Age of Mackenzie King. Toronto: James Lorimer, 1976. (First published 1955).

Forcese, Dennis
The Canadian Class Structure. Series in Canadian Sociology. Toronto: McGraw-Hill Ryerson, 1975.

CLASS CONFLICT (cont'd)

Forsey, Eugene
The History of Canadian Trade Unionism, 1812-1902. Montreal: McGill-Queen's University Press, 1973.

The Canadian Labour Movement 1812-1902. Historical Booklet, no. 27. Ottawa: Canadian Historical Association, 1974.

Garner, Hugh
Cabbagetown. Toronto: Ryerson Press, 1968. (First published 1950).

Gonick, Cy
Inflation or Depression: The Continuing Crisis of the Canadian Economy. Toronto: James Lorimer, 1975.

"Poverty and Capitalism." Poverty and Social Policy in Canada. Edited by W.E. Mann. Vancouver: Copp Clark, 1970.

Grove, Frederick Philip
The Master of the Mill. Toronto: McClelland and Stewart, 1961.

Hamilton, Richard, and Pinard, Maurice
"Poverty in Canada: Illusion and Reality." Canadian Review of Sociology and Anthropology 14:2 (May 1977):247-252.

Hann, Russell; Kealey, Gregory; Kealey, Linda; and Warrian, Peter
Primary Sources in Canadian Working Class History, 1860-1930. Kitchener: Dumont Press, 1973.

Harney, Robert, and Troper, Harold
Immigrants: A Portrait of the Urban Experience, 1890-1930. Toronto: Van Nostrand Reinhold, 1975.

Harp, John, and Hofley, John R., eds.
Poverty in Canada. Scarborough, Ont.: Prentice-Hall, 1971.

Harvey, F., ed.
Aspects historiques du mouvement ouvrier au Québec. Etudes d'histoire du Québec, 6. Montréal: Editions du Boréal Express, 1973.

Horowitz, Gad
Canadian Labour in Politics. Studies in the Structure of Power: Decision-Making in Canada, 4. Toronto: University of Toronto Press, 1968.

Hutcheson, John
"Class and Income Distribution in Canada." Canada Ltd.: The Political Economy of Dependency, pp. 57-83. Edited by Robert Laxer. Toronto: McClelland and Stewart, 1973.

CLASS CONFLICT (cont'd)

Innis, Harold
"Labour in Canadian Economic History." Essays in Canadian Economic History, pp. 176-199. Edited by Mary Q. Innis. Toronto: University of Toronto Press, 1969. (First published 1956).

Isbester, Fraser, and Miller, Richard, eds.
Canadian Labour in Transition. Scarborough, Ont.: Prentice-Hall, 1971.

Jamieson, Stuart
Industrial Relations in Canada. Studies in International Labor. Ithaca: Cornell University Press, 1957.

Times of Trouble: Labour Unrest and Industrial Conflict in Canada, 1900-1966. Study no. 22. Ottawa: Task Force on Labour Relations, 1968.

Johnson, Leo A.
"The Development of Class in Canada in the Twentieth Century." Capitalism and the National Question in Canada, pp. 141-183. Edited by G. Teeple. Toronto: University of Toronto Press, 1972.

Poverty in Wealth: The Capitalist Labour Market and Income Distribution in Canada. Rev. ed. Toronto: New Hogtown Press, 1974.

"Illusions or Realities: Hamilton and Pinard's Approach to Poverty." Canadian Review of Sociology and Anthropology 14:3 (August 1977):341-346.

Johnston, Walter, ed.
Working in Canada. Montreal: Black Rose Books, 1976.

Jordan, Mary V.
Survival: Labour's Trials and Tribulations in Canada. Toronto: McDonald House, 1975.

Kealey, Greg, ed.
Canada Investigates Industrialism: The Royal Commission on the Relations of Labour and Capital 1889. Toronto: University of Toronto Press, 1973.

Working Class Toronto at the Turn of the Century. Toronto: New Hogtown Press, 1975.

"'The Honest Workingman' and Workers' Control: The Experience of Toronto Skilled Workers, 1860-1892." Labour/Le Travailleur 1 (1976):32-68.

CLASS CONFLICT (cont'd)

Kealey, Greg, and Warrian, Peter, eds.,
Essays in Canadian Working Class History. Canadian Social History series. Toronto: McClelland and Stewart, 1976.

King, W.L. Mackenzie
Industry and Humanity: A Study in the Principles Underlying Industrial Reconstruction. Toronto: University of Toronto Press, 1973. (First published 1918).

Knight, Rolf, and Knight, Phyllis
A Very Ordinary Life. Vancouver: New Star Books, 1974.

Kwavnick, David
Organized Labour and Pressure Politics: The Canadian Labour Congress, 1956-1968. Montreal: McGill-Queen's University Press, 1972.

Lang, John
"The Million Dollar Question: The CLC and Canadian Unions." This Magazine 7:2 (August 1973):19-22.

Langdon, Steven
The Emergence of the Canadian Working-Class Movement, 1845-75. Toronto: New Hogtown Press, 1973.

Laxer, Robert
Canada's Unions. Toronto: James Lorimer, 1976.

Lazarus, Morden
Years of Hard Labour: An Account of the Canadian Workingman, His Organizations and Tribulations Over a Period of More Than a Hundred Years. Don Mills, Ont.: Ontario Federation of Labour, 1974.

LeBlanc, A., and Thwaites, James
Le monde ouvrier au Québec: bibliographie rétrospective. Collection Histoire des travailleurs québécois, 1. Montreal: Les Presses de l'Université du Québec, 1973.

Leyton, Elliott
Dying Hard: The Ravages of Industrial Carnage. Toronto: McClelland and Stewart, 1975.

Lipton, C.
The Trade Union Movement of Canada 1827-1959. Toronto: NC Press, 1973. (First published 1967).

Liversedge, Ronald
Recollections of the On-To-Ottawa Trek. The Carleton Library, no. 66. Toronto: McClelland and Stewart, 1973. (First published 1963).

CLASS CONFLICT (cont'd)

Logan, H.A.
Trade Unions in Canada: Their Development and Functioning. Toronto: Macmillan, 1948.

State Intervention and Assistance in Collective Bargaining: The Canadian Experience, 1943-1954. Canadian Studies in Economics, 6. Toronto: University of Toronto Press, 1956.

Macleod, Catherine
"Women in Production: The Toronto Dressmakers' Strike in 1931." Women at Work: Ontario, 1850-1930, pp. 309-329. Edited by Janice Acton, et al. Toronto: Canadian Women's Educational Press, 1974.

Mann, W.E., ed.
Poverty and Social Policy in Canada. Vancouver: Copp Clark, 1970.

Mannion, John
Irish Settlement in Eastern Canada: A Study of Cultural Transfer and Adaptation. Department of Geography. Research publication, no. 12. Toronto: University of Toronto Press, 1974.

Manuel, George, and Posluns, M.
The Fourth World: An Indian Reality. Don Mills, Ont.: Collier-Macmillan, 1974.

Manzer, R.
Canada: A Socio-Political Report. Series in Canadian Politics. Toronto: McGraw-Hill Ryerson, 1974.

Marlyn, John
Under the Ribs of Death. Toronto: McClelland and Stewart, 1957.

Marshall, Stan
"Embourgeoisement or Proletarianization?" Alternate Routes 1 (1977): 58-86.

Martell, George
"Downtown Kids Aren't Dumb: They Need a Better Program." The Politics of the Canadian Public School, pp. 39-64. Edited by G. Martell. Toronto: James, Lewis and Samuel, 1974.

Maslove, A.
The Pattern of Taxation in Canada. Ottawa: Information Canada, 1972.

Masters, D.C.
The Winnipeg General Strike. Social Credit in Alberta: Its Background and Development, 2. Toronto: University of Toronto Press, 1950.

CLASS CONFLICT (cont'd)

Mayer, Jan
"Social Mobility: Current Thrusts (and Non-Thrusts): A Critical Approach to the Analysis of Mobility." Alternate Routes 1 (1977): 87-102.

McCormack, A. Ross
"The Blanketstiffs: Itinerant Railway Construction Workers, 1896-1914." Canada's Visual History, Series 1 (slides).

McDermott, Pat
"Oil Companies Engulf Stations: What's Behind Self-Serve?" Ontario Report 2:5 (January 1978):18-20.

McEwen, Tom
The Forge Glows Red: From Blacksmith to Revolutionary. Toronto: Progress Books, 1974.

McKenzie, Ruth
"Proletarian Literature in Canada." Dalhousie Review 19 (April 1939).

Eight Men Speak and Other Communist Plays of the 1930's. Toronto: New Hogtown Press, 1976.

McNaught, Kenneth
A Prophet in Politics: A Biography of J.S. Woodsworth. Toronto: University of Toronto Press, 1959.

McNaught, Kenneth, and Bercuson, David
The Winnipeg Strike: 1919. Don Mills, Ont.: Longmans, 1974.

Mealing, S.R.
"The Concept of Social Class and the Interpretation of Canadian History." Canadian Historical Review 46:3 (September 1965):201-218.

Neary, P.
"Bell Island: A Newfoundland Mining Community, 1896-1966." Canada's Visual History, Series 1 (slides).

Palmer, Bryan D.
"Most Uncommon Common Men: Craft and Culture in Historical Perspective." Labour/Le Travailleur 1 (1976):5-31.

Panitch, Leo
"Wage and Price Controls." This Magazine 10:1 (February 1976):4-7.

"Labour's Manifesto." This Magazine 10:5-6 (November-December 1976):9-11.

Panting, G.E.
"The Fishermen's Protective Union of Newfoundland and the Farmers' Organizations in Western Canada." Canadian Historical Association Report (1963):141-151.

Peitchinis, Stephen G.
The Canadian Labour Market. Toronto: Oxford University Press, 1975.

Penner, Norman, ed.
Winnipeg 1919: The Strikers' Own History of the Winnipeg General Strike. Toronto: James, Lewis and Samuel, 1973.

Pentland, H.C.
"The Lachine Strike of 1843." Canadian Historical Review 29:3 (September 1948):255-277.

"The Development of a Capitalistic Labour Market in Canada." Canadian Journal of Economics and Political Science 25:4 (November 1959):450-461.

A Study of the Changing Social, Economic and Political Background of the Canadian System of Industrial Relations. Ottawa: Task Force in Labour Relations, 1968. (Available only in university libraries.)

Phillips, Paul A.
No Power Greater: A Century of Labour in British Columbia. Vancouver: B.C. Federation of Labour, 1967.

"The British Columbia Mining Frontier, 1880-1920." Canada's Visual History, Series 1 (slides).

"Canadian Labour and the New Industrial State." Nationalism, Technology and the Future of Canada, pp. 123-145. Edited by Wallace Gagne. Toronto: Macmillan, 1976.

Pike, Robert M.
Who Doesn't Get to University--and Why: A Study on Accessibility to Higher Education in Canada. Ottawa: Association of Universities and Colleges of Canada, 1970.

Pinard, Maurice
"Working Class Politics: An Interpretation of the Quebec Case." Canadian Review of Sociology and Anthropology 7:2 (May 1970): 87-109.

Podoluk, Jenny R.
Income of Canadians. Ottawa: Dominion Bureau of Statistics, 1968.

Porter, John
The Vertical Mosaic: An Analysis of Social Class and Power in Canada. Studies in the Structure of Power: Decision-Making in Canada, no. 2. Toronto: University of Toronto Press, 1965.

Porter, Marion; Porter, John; and Blishen, Bernard
Does Money Matter? Prospects for Higher Education. Toronto: York University Institute for Behavioural Research, 1973.

Pryke, Ken
"Labour and Politics: Nova Scotia at Confederation." Social History 6 (November 1970):33-55.

Rapoport, Roger
"The Educator as Pusher: I. Just a Little Pill to Keep the Kids Quiet?" The Politics of the Canadian Public School, pp. 71-74. Edited by G. Martell. Toronto: James, Lewis and Samuel, 1974.

Rawlyk, George
"The Farmer-Labour Movement and the Failure of Socialism in Nova Scotia." Essays on the Left: Essays in Honour of T.C. Douglas, pp. 31-41. Edited by L. Lapierre. Toronto: McClelland and Stewart, 1971.

Rinehart, James W.
The Tyranny of Work. Canadian Social Problems series. Don Mills, Ont.: Longmans, 1975.

Rinehart, James W., and Okraku, I.
"A Study of Class Consciousness." Canadian Review of Sociology and Anthropology 11:3 (August 1974): 197-213.

Robin, Martin
"Registration, Conscription and Independent Labour Politics, 1916-1917." Canadian Historical Review 47:2 (June 1966):101-118.

"The TLC and Political Action, 1899-1908." Relations Industrielles/Industrial Relations 22 (1967).

Radical Politics and Canadian Labour, 1880-1930. Research series, 7. Kingston: Industrial Relations Centre, Queen's University, 1968.

Rodney, William
Soldiers of the International: A History of the Communist Party of Canada, 1919-1929. Canadian Studies in History and Government, 10. Toronto: University of Toronto Press, 1968.

CLASS CONFLICT (cont'd)

Rouillard, Jacques
Les travailleurs du coton au Québec, 1900-1915. Collection Histoire des travaillers québécois, 3. Montréal: Les Presses de l'Université du Québec, 1974.

"Marie Blanchet, Valleyfield Cotton Weaver in 1909." Canada's Visual History, Series 1 (slides).

Ryerson, Stanley
"Quebec: Concepts of Class and Nation." Capitalism and the National Question in Canada, pp. 211-227. Edited by G. Teeple. Toronto: University of Toronto Press, 1972.

St. Pierre, J.
"The Asbestos Strike, 1949." Canada's Visual History, Series 1 (slides).

Scott, Bruce
"Cultivating the Worker's Smile: Works Councils in Canada." This Magazine 11:1 (January-February 1977):30-33.

Scott, F., et al.
Social Planning for Canada. The Social History of Canada, 26. Toronto: University of Toronto Press, 1975. (First published 1935).

Scott, Jack
Plunderbund and Proletariat. Vancouver: New Star Books, 1975.

Sweat and Struggle: Working Class Struggles in Canada. Vol. I: 1789-1899. Vancouver: New Star Books, 1974.

Scott, J., and Howard, R.
"International Unions and the Ideology of Class Collaboration." Capitalism and the National Question in Canada, pp. 67-87. Edited by G. Teeple. Toronto: University of Toronto Press, 1972.

Seymour, Edward
An Illustrated History of Canadian Labour, 1800-1974. Ottawa: Canadian Labour Congress, 1976.

Smith, Dorothy E.
"Women, the Family and Corporate Capitalism." Women in Canada, pp. 2-35. Edited by Marylee Stephenson. Toronto: New Press, 1973.

Smith, Douglas A.
"The Determinants of Strike Activity in Canada." Relations Industrielles/Industrial Relations 27:4 (1974).

CLASS CONFLICT (cont'd)

Souchotte, Sandra
"Workers' Theatre in the Thirties: Part I." This Magazine 9:2 (May-June 1975):3-6.

"Workers' Theatre in the Thirties: Part II." This Magazine 9:3 (July-August 1975):3-5.

Stelter, G.A.
"The Northern Ontario Mining Frontier, 1880-1920." Canada's Visual History, Series 1 (slides).

Stevenson, Paul
"Class and Left-Wing Radicalism." Canadian Review of Sociology and Anthropology 14:3 (August 1977):269-284.

Thompson, Thomas Phillips
The Politics of Labour. Toronto: University of Toronto Press, 1975. (First published 1887).

Trudeau, Pierre Elliott, ed.
The Asbestos Strike. Toronto: James, Lewis and Samuel, 1974. (First published 1956).

Vanderkamp, John
"Economic Activity and Strikes in Canada." Relations Industrielles/ Industrial Relations 9:1 (1969).

Watkins, Mel
"The Trade Union Movement in Canada." Canada Ltd.: The Political Economy of Dependency, pp. 178-196. Edited by Robert Laxer. Toronto: McClelland and Stewart, 1973.

Watt, F.W.
"The National Policy, the Workingman and Proletarian Ideas in Victorian Canada." Canadian Historical Review 40:1 (March 1959): 1-26.

"Literature of Protest." Literary History of Canada: Canadian Literature in English, 2nd ed., Vol. I, pp. 473-489. Edited by C.F. Klinck. Toronto: University of Toronto Press, 1976.

Woywitka, Anne B.
"Drumheller Strike of 1919." Alberta Historical Review 21:1 (Winter 1973):1-7.

"Strike at Waterways." Alberta Historical Review 20:4 (Autumn 1972):1-5.

CLASS CONFLICT (cont'd)

Wright, Richard, and Endres, Robin, eds.
'Eight Men Speak' and Other Plays From the Canadian Workers' Theatre. Toronto: New Hogtown Press, 1976.

Zwelling, Marc
The Strikebreakers: The Report of the Strikebreaking Committee of the Ontario Federation of Labour and the Labour Council of Metropolitan Toronto. Toronto: New Press, 1972.

V. THE NATURE OF THE CANADIAN STATE

1. STATE POLICY AND POLITICS

Aitken, Hugh G.J., ed.
The State and Economic Growth: Papers. New York: Social Science Research Council, 1959.

Armitage, Andrew
Social Welfare in Canada: Ideals and Realities. Toronto: McClelland and Stewart, 1975.

Armstrong, Hugh
"The Labour Force and State Workers in Canada." The Canadian State: Political Economy and Political Power, pp. 289-210. Edited by Leo Panitch. Toronto: University of Toronto Press, 1977.

Avery, Donald, and Neary, Peter
"Laurier, Borden and a White British Columbia." Journal of Canadian Studies 12:4 (Summer 1977):24-34.

Badgley, Robin F., and Wolfe, Samuel
Doctors' Strike: Medical Care and Conflict in Saskatchewan. Toronto: Macmillan, 1967.

Bercuson, D.J.
Canada and the Burden of Unity. Toronto: Macmillan, 1977.

Brewis, T.N.
Regional Economic Policies in Canada. Toronto: Macmillan, 1969.

Canada. Economic Council
Living Together: A Study of Regional Disparities. Ottawa: Supply and Services, 1977.

Canada. Economic Council
Second Annual Review. Ottawa: Queen's Printer, 1965.

Clarkson, Stephen, ed.
An Independent Foreign Policy for Canada? A Carleton Contemporary. Toronto: McClelland and Stewart, 1968.

Corbett, D.C.
Canada's Immigration Policy: A Critique. Toronto: University of Toronto Press, 1957.

Deaton, Rick
"The Fiscal Crisis of the State and the Revolt of the Public Employee." Our Generation 8:4 (October 1972):11-51.

STATE POLICY AND POLITICS (cont'd)

Dosman, Edgar J.
The National Interest: The Politics of Northern Development, 1968-75. Toronto: McClelland and Stewart, 1975.

Eayrs, James
In Defense of Canada. 2 vols. Studies in the Structure of Power: Decision-Making in Canada, 1+3. Toronto: University of Toronto Press, 1965, 1967.

Endres, Robin
"Art and Accumulation: The Canadian State and the Business of Art." The Canadian State: Political Economy and Political Power, pp. 417-445. Edited by Leo Panitch. Toronto: University of Toronto Press, 1977.

Finkel, Alvin
"Origins of the Welfare State in Canada." The Canadian State: Political Economy and Political Power, pp. 344-370. Edited by Leo Panitch. Toronto: University of Toronto Press, 1977.

Granatstein, J.L.
Canadian Foreign Policy Since 1945: Middle Power or Satellite? Issues in Canadian History. Toronto: Copp Clark, 1965.

Canada's War: The Politics of the Mackenzie King Government, 1939-1945. Toronto: Oxford University Press, 1975.

Hill, O. Mary
Canada's Salesman to the World: The Department of Trade and Commerce, 1892-1939. Montreal: McGill-Queen's University Press, 1977.

Hodgetts, J.E.
The Canadian Public Service: A Physiology of Government, 1867-1970. Studies in the Structure of Power: Decision-Making in Canada. Toronto: University of Toronto Press, 1973.

Pioneer Public Service: An Administrative History of the United Canadas, 1841-1867. Canadian Government series, 7. Toronto: University of Toronto Press, 1955.

Hodgetts, J.E.; McCloskey, William; Whitaker, Reginald; and Wilson, V. Seymour
The Biography of an Institution: The Civil Service Commission of Canada, 1908-1967. Canadian Public Administration series. Montreal: McGill-Queen's University Press, 1972.

STATE POLICY AND POLITICS (cont'd)

Hutcheson, John
"The Capitalist State in Canada." Canada Ltd.: The Political Economy of Dependency, pp. 153-177. Edited by Robert Laxer. Toronto: McClelland and Stewart, 1973.

Innis, H.A.
Political Economy in the Modern State. Toronto: Ryerson Press, 1946.

Kalbach, Warren S.
The Impact of Immigration on Canada's Population. Ottawa: Dominion Bureau of Statistics, 1970.

Kennedy, J.
History of the Department of Munitions and Supply: Canada in the Second World War. 2 vols. Ottawa: King's Printer, 1950.

League for Social Reconstruction
Social Planning for Canada. The Social History of Canada, 26. Toronto: University of Toronto Press, 1975. (First published 1935).

Loney, Martin
"A Political Economy of Citizen Participation." The Canadian State: Political Economy and Political Power, pp. 446-472. Edited by Leo Panitch. Toronto: University of Toronto Press, 1977.

Mackintosh, W.A.
"The White Paper on Employment and Income in Its 1945 Setting." Canadian Economic Policy Since the War. Edited by S.F. Kaliski. Montreal: Private Planning Association of Canada, 1966.

Mahon, Rianne
"Canadian Public Policy: The Unequal Structure of Representation." The Canadian State: Political Economy and Political Power, pp. 165-198. Edited by Leo Panitch. Toronto: University of Toronto Press, 1977.

Martell, George
"The Schools, the State and the Corporations." The Politics of the Canadian Public School, pp. 1-36. Edited by George Martell. Toronto: James Lorimer, 1974.

Morton, Desmond
"Aid to the Civil Power: The Canadian Militia in Support of Social Order, 1867-1914." Studies in Canadian Social History, pp. 417-434. Edited by Michiel Horn and Ronald Sabourin. Toronto: McClelland and Stewart, 1974. Reprinted from Canadian Historical Review 51:4 (December 1970):407-425.

STATE POLICY AND POLITICS (cont'd)

Oliver, M., ed.
Social Purpose for Canada. Toronto: University of Toronto Press, 1961.

Olsen, Dennis
"The State Elites." The Canadian State: Political Economy and Political Power, pp. 199-224. Edited by Leo Panitch. Toronto: University of Toronto Press, 1977.

Panitch, Leo
"The Role and Nature of the Canadian State." The Canadian State: Political Economy and Political Power, pp. 3-27. Edited by Leo Panitch. Toronto: University of Toronto Press, 1977.

Panitch, Leo, ed.
The Canadian State: Political Economy and Political Power. Toronto: University of Toronto Press, 1977.

"The Development of Corporatism in Liberal Democracies." Comparative Political Studies 10:1 (April 1977):61-90.

Porter, John
"Power and Freedom in Canadian Democracy." Social Purpose for Canada, pp. 27-56. Edited by M. Oliver. Toronto: University of Toronto Press, 1961.

Pratt, Larry
"The State and Province-Building: Alberta's Development Strategy." The Canadian State: Political Economy and Political Power, pp. 133-162. Edited by Leo Panitch. Toronto: University of Toronto Press, 1977.

Prentice, Alison
The School Promoters: Education and Social Class in Mid-Nineteenth Century Upper Canada. Toronto: McClelland and Stewart, 1978.

Reynolds, Lloyd G.
The Control of Competition in Canada. Harvard Studies in Monopoly and Competition, 2. Cambridge, Mass.: Harvard University Press, 1977.

Rosenbluth, Gideon
The Canadian Economy and Disarmament. The Carleton Library, no. 113. Toronto: McClelland and Stewart, 1978. (First published 1967).

Schecter, Stephen
"Urban Politics in Capitalist Society: A Revolutionary Strategy." Our Generation 11:1 (Fall 1975):28-41.

Schecter, Stephen
"Capitalism, Class and Educational Reform in Canada." The Canadian State: Political Economy and Political Power, pp. 373-416. Edited by Leo Panitch. Toronto: University of Toronto Press, 1977.

Scott, F., et al.
Social Planning for Canada. The Social History of Canada, 26. Toronto: University of Toronto Press, 1975. (First published 1935).

Smiley, Donald
The Canadian Political Nationality. Rev. ed. Toronto: Methuen, 1970.

Smith, Denis
Bleeding Hearts...Bleeding Country: Canada and the Quebec Crisis. Edmonton: M.G. Hurtig, 1971.

Stevenson, Garth
"Federalism and the Political Economy of the Canadian State." The Canadian State: Political Economy and Political Power, pp. 71-100. Edited by Leo Panitch. Toronto: University of Toronto Press, 1977.

Swartz, Donald
"The Health Industry." This Magazine 10:3 (June-July 1976):30-34.

Thompson, John Herd
The Harvests of War: The Prairie West, 1914-1918. The Canadian Social History series. Toronto: McClelland and Stewart, 1978.

Wolfe, David
"The State and Economic Policy in Canada, 1968-75." The Canadian State: Political Economy and Political Power, pp. 251-288. Edited by Leo Panitch. Toronto: University of Toronto Press, 1977.

"Economic Growth and Foreign Investment: A Perspective on Canadian Economic Policy." Journal of Canadian Studies 13:1 (Spring 1978): 3-20.

Younge, Eva R.
"Population Movements and the Assimilation of Alien Groups in Canada." Canadian Journal of Economics and Political Science 10:3 (August 1944):372-380.

2. POLITICAL PARTIES

Abella, Irving
Nationalism, Communism and Canadian Labour: The CIO, the Communist Party, and the Canadian Congress of Labour, 1935-1956. Toronto: University of Toronto Press, 1973.

Allan, Ted, and Gordon, Sydney
The Scalpel, the Sword: The Story of Dr. Norman Bethune. Toronto: McClelland and Stewart, 1971.

Allen, Richard
The Social Passion: Religion and Social Reform in Canada, 1914-1928. Toronto: University of Toronto Press, 1971.

Avakumovic, Ivan
The Communist Party in Canada: A History. Toronto: McClelland and Stewart, 1975.

Socialism in Canada: A Study of the CCF-NDP in Federal and Provincial Politics. Toronto: McClelland and Stewart, 1978.

Beck, J.M.
Pendulum of Power: Canada's Federal Elections. Scarborough, Ont.: Prentice-Hall, 1968.

Buck, Tim
Our Fight for Canada: Selected Writings (1923-1959). Toronto: Progress Books, 1959.

Canada: The Communist Viewpoint. Toronto: Progress Books, 1948.

Lenin and Canada: His Influence on Canadian Political Life. Toronto: Progress Books, 1970.

Thirty Years, 1922-1952: The Story of the Communist Movement. Toronto: Progress Books, 1952.

Canadian Dimension
"The NDP and the Waffle." (Special Supplement) 7:8 (April 1971).

Chi, N.H.
"Class Voting in Canadian Politics." The Canadian Political Process: A Reader. Rev. ed., pp. 226-247. Edited by O.S. Kruhlack, et al. Toronto: Holt, Rinehart and Winston, 1973.

Conway, John
"Populism in the United States, Russia, and Canada: Explaining the Roots of Canada's Third Parties." Canadian Journal of Political Science 9:1 (March 1978):99-124.

POLITICAL PARTIES (cont'd)

Creighton, D.
John A. Macdonald: The Old Chieftain. Vol. II. Toronto: Macmillan, 1955.

Cross, Michael
The Decline and Fall of a Good Idea: CCF-NDP Manifestoes, 1932-1969. Toronto: New Hogtown Press, 1974.

Dafoe, J.W.
Clifford Sifton in Relation to His Times. Toronto: Macmillan, 1931.

Laurier: A Study in Canadian Politics. The Carleton Library, no. 3. Toronto: McClelland and Stewart, 1963. (First published 1922).

Dion, L.
"Participation in the Political Process." Queen's Quarterly, 75 (Autumn 1968).

English, John
The Decline of Politics: The Conservatives and the Party System 1901-20. Canadian Government series. Toronto: University of Toronto Press, 1977.

Ferns, Henry, and Ostry, Bernard
The Age of Mackenzie King. Toronto: James Lorimer, 1976. (First published 1955).

Gonick, Cy
"Schreyer's New Democrats." Canadian Dimension 9:6 (1973).

"Socialism and the Economics of Growthmanship." Essays on the Left: Essays in Honour of T.C. Douglas, pp. 135-159. Edited by L. Lapierre, et al. Toronto: McClelland and Stewart, 1971.

Graham, R.
Arthur Meighen. Toronto: Clarke Irwin, 1960.

Granatstein, J.L.
The Politics of Survival: The Conservative Party of Canada, 1939-1945. Toronto: University of Toronto Press, 1967.

Canada's War: The Politics of the Mackenzie King Government, 1939-45. Toronto: Oxford University Press, 1975.

Horowitz, Gad
"Tories, Socialists and the Demise of Canada." Canadian Dimension 23 (1965).

POLITICAL PARTIES (cont'd)

Horowitz, Gad

Canadian Labour in Politics. Studies in the Structure of Power: Decision-Making in Canada, 4. Toronto: University of Toronto Press, 1968.

"Conservativism, Liberalism, and Socialism in Canada: An Interpretation." Canada: A Sociological Profile, 2nd ed., pp. 8-23. Edited by W.E. Mann. Toronto: Copp Clark, 1971. Original in Canadian Journal of Economics and Political Science 32:2 (May 1966):143-171.

Irving, John

The Social Credit Movement in Alberta. Social Credit in Alberta: Its Background and Development, 10. Toronto: University of Toronto Press, 1959.

Kilbourn, William

Pipeline: TransCanada and the Great Debate: A History of Business and Politics. Toronto: Clarke Irwin, 1970.

LaMarsh, Judy

Memoirs of a Bird in a Gilded Cage. Toronto: McClelland and Stewart, 1969.

Lewis, David

Louder Voices: The Corporate Welfare Bums. Toronto: James, Lewis and Samuel, 1972.

Lipset, Seymour Martin

Agrarian Socialism: The Cooperative Commonwealth Federation in Saskatchewan; A Study in Political Sociology. Rev. ed. Berkeley: University of California Press, 1971. (First published 1950).

Macpherson, C.B.

Democracy in Alberta: Social Credit and the Party System. 2nd ed. Toronto: University of Toronto Press, 1968. (First edition 1955).

Democratic Theory: Essays in Retrieval. Oxford: Clarendon Press, 1973.

"Politics: Post-Liberal-Democracy?" Ideology in Social Science: Readings in Critical Social Theory, pp. 17-31. Edited by Robin Blackburn. New York: Vintage, 1973. (First published 1964).

The Real World of Democracy. The Massey Lectures, 4th series. Toronto: CBC Publications, 1965.

Mallory, J.R.

Social Credit and the Federal Power in Canada. Social Credit in Alberta: Its Background and Development, 5. Toronto: University of Toronto Press, 1977. (First published 1954).

POLITICAL PARTIES (cont'd)

McKenty, Neil
Mitch Hepburn. Toronto: McClelland and Stewart, 1967.

McNaught, Kenneth
A Prophet in Politics: A Biography of J.S. Woodsworth. Toronto: University of Toronto Press, 1959.

McQuarrie, Heath
The Conservative Party. Toronto: McClelland and Stewart, 1965.

Meisel, J.
Working Papers on Canadian Politics. Enl. ed. Montreal: McGill-Queen's University Press, 1973.

Papers on the 1962 Election. Toronto: University of Toronto Press, 1964.

"Canadian Parties and Politics." Contemporary Canada, pp. 124-147. Edited by R.H. Leach. Toronto: University of Toronto Press, 1968.

Menzies, J.
"Votes for Saskatchewan Women." Politics in Saskatchewan, pp. 78-92. Edited by Norman Ward and Duff Spafford. Toronto: Longmans, 1969.

Morton, W.L.
The Progressive Party in Canada. Social Credit in Alberta: Its Background and Development, 1. Toronto: University of Toronto Press, 1950.

Naylor, R.T.
"The Ideological Foundations of Social Democracy and Social Credit." Capitalism and the National Question in Canada, pp. 251-256. Edited by G. Teeple. Toronto: University of Toronto Press, 1972.

Newman, Peter
Renegade in Power: The Diefenbaker Years. The Carleton Library, no. 70. Toronto: McClelland and Stewart, 1973.

Distemper of Our Times; Canadian Politics in Transition: 1963-1968. Toronto: McClelland and Stewart, 1968.

Ostry, Bernard
"Conservatives, Liberals and Labour in the 1870's." Canadian Historical Review 41:2 (June 1960):93-127.

POLITICAL PARTIES (cont'd)

Paltiel, K.Z.
Political Party Financing in Canada. Series in Canadian Politics. Toronto: McGraw-Hill, 1970.

Penner, Norman
The Canadian Left: A Critical Analysis. Scarborough, Ont.: Prentice-Hall, 1977.

Pinard, Maurice
The Rise of a Third Party: A Study in Crisis Politics. Scarborough, Ont.: Prentice-Hall, 1971.

Pross, A. Paul, ed.
Pressure Group Behaviour in Canadian Politics. Series in Canadian Politics. Scarborough: McGraw-Hill Ryerson, 1975.

Quinn, Herbert
The Union Nationale: A Study in Quebec Nationalism. Toronto: University of Toronto Press, 1963.

Ryan, Oscar
Tim Buck: A Conscience for Canada. Toronto: Progress Books, 1975.

Saywell, John
The Rise of the Parti Quebecois, 1967-1976. Toronto: University of Toronto Press, 1977.

Sharp, Paul F.
The Agrarian Revolt in Western Canada: A Survey Showing American Parallels. Minneapolis: University of Minnesota Press, 1948.

Smart, John
"Populist and Socialist Movements in Canadian History." Canada, Ltd.: The Political Economy of Dependency, pp. 197-212. Edited by Robert Laxer. Toronto: McClelland and Stewart, 1973.

Smith, Albert Edward
All My Life: An Autobiography. Toronto: Progress Books, 1977. (First published 1949).

Thomson, Dale
Louis St-Laurent: Canadian. Toronto: Macmillan, 1967.

Thorburn, Hugh, ed.
Party Politics in Canada. 2nd ed. Scarborough: Prentice-Hall, 1967.

"Pressure Groups in Canadian Politics." Canadian Journal of Political Science 30:2 (May 1964).

POLITICAL PARTIES (cont'd)

Underhill, Frank
In Search of Canadian Liberalism. Toronto: Macmillan, 1960.

Wise, S.F.
"Conservatism and Political Development: The Canadian Case." South Atlantic Quarterly 64 (Spring 1970).

Wood, Louis Aubrey
A History of Farmers' Movements in Canada. The Social History of Canada, 25. Toronto: University of Toronto Press, 1975. (First published 1924).

Young, Walter D.
The Anatomy of a Party: The National C.C.F., 1932-61. Toronto: University of Toronto Press, 1969.

Zakuta, Leo
A Protest Movement Becalmed: A Study of Change in the CCF. Canadian Studies in Sociology. Toronto: University of Toronto Press, 1964.

3. CONFEDERATION, NATIONAL POLICY, AND DOMINION-PROVINCIAL RELATIONS

Acheson, T.W.
"The National Policy and the Industrialization of the Maritimes, 1880-1910." Acadiensis 1 (Spring 1972).

Bailey, A.G.
"The Basis and Persistence of Opposition to Confederation in New Brunswick." Culture and Nationality, pp. 93-117. The Carleton Library, no. 58. Toronto: McClelland and Stewart, 1972.

"New Brunswick: Keystone of the Arch." Culture and Nationality, pp. 118-127. The Carleton Library, no. 58. Toronto: McClelland and Stewart, 1972.

Barber, C.L.
"Canadian Tariff Policy." Canadian Journal of Economics and Political Science 21:4 (November 1955):513-530.

Beck, J. Murray, ed.
Joseph Howe: Voice of Nova Scotia; A Selection. The Carleton Library, no. 20. Toronto: McClelland and Stewart, 1964.

Bliss, Michael
"Canadianizing American Business: The Roots of the Branch Plant." Close the 49th Parallel, Etc.: The Americanization of Canada, pp. 27-42. Edited by Ian Lumsden. Toronto: University of Toronto Press, 1970.

Buckley, Kenneth
Capital Formation in Canada, 1896-1930. The Carleton Library, no. 77. Toronto: McClelland and Stewart, 1970. (First published 1955).

Canada. Royal Commission on Bilingualism and Biculturalism
Report. Ottawa: Information Canada, 1969.

Corry, J.A.
Difficulties of Divided Jurisdiction. Royal Commission on Dominion-Provincial Relations Report, Appendix 7. Ottawa: King's Printer, 1939.

Growth of Government Activities Since Confederation. Royal Commission on Dominion-Provincial Relations. Ottawa: King's Printer, 1939.

Cowan, Helen I.
British Emigration to British North America: The First Hundred Years. Rev. and enl. ed. Toronto: University of Toronto Press, 1961.

CONFEDERATION, NATIONAL POLICY, AND DOMINION-PROVINCIAL RELATIONS (cont'd)

Creighton, D.G.

British North America at Confederation. Royal Commission on Dominion-Provincial Relations Report, Appendix 2. Ottawa: King's Printer, 1939.

John A. Macdonald: The Old Chieftain. Vol. II. Toronto: Macmillan, 1955.

"The Economic Background of the Rebellions of 1837." Towards the Discovery of Canada, pp. 103-121. Toronto: Macmillan, 1972.

"The Victorians and the Empire." Towards the Discovery of Canada, pp. 137-156. Toronto: Macmillan, 1972.

"Economic Nationalism and Confederation." Towards the Discovery of Canada, pp. 122-136. Toronto: Macmillan, 1972.

Empire of the St. Lawrence. Toronto: Macmillan, 1956. (First published 1937).

Cross, Michael

"Stony Monday, 1849: The Rebellion Losses Riots in Bytown." Ontario History 63 (September 1971):177.

Dales, John

"Some Historical and Theoretical Comment on Canada's National Policies." Queen's Quarterly 71 (Autumn 1964).

Dubuc, Alfred

"The Decline of Confederation and the New Nationalism." Nationalism in Canada, pp. 112-132. Edited by Peter Russell. Toronto: McGraw-Hill, 1966.

Fowke, V.C.

"The National Policy--Old and New." Canadian Journal of Economics and Political Science 18:3 (August 1952):271-286.

"National Policy and Western Development in North America." Journal of Economic History 16:4 (December 1956):461-479.

The National Policy and the Wheat Economy. Social Credit in Alberta: Its Background and Development, no. 7. Toronto: University of Toronto Press, 1957.

Harris, R., and Warkentin, John

Canada Before Confederation: A Study in Historical Geography. Toronto: Oxford University Press, 1974.

Howard, Joseph Kinsey
Strange Empire: Louis Riel and the Métis People. Toronto: James, Lewis and Samuel, 1974. (First published 1952).

Landon, Fred
Western Ontario and the American Frontier. The Carleton Library, no. 34. Toronto: McClelland and Stewart, 1967.

Macdonald, Norman
Canada 1763-1841: Immigration and Settlement; the Administration of the Imperial Land Regulations. London: Longmans, Green, 1939.

Canada: Immigration and Colonization, 1841-1903. Toronto: Macmillan, 1966.

Mackintosh, W.A.
The Economic Background of Dominion-Provincial Relations. Royal Commission Report on Dominion-Provincial Relations, Appendix III. Ottawa: King's Printer, 1938. Reprinted by McClelland and Stewart: The Carleton Library, no. 13. Edited by J.H. Dales. Toronto: 1964.

"Economic Factors in Canadian History." Approaches to Canadian Economic History: A Selection of Essays, pp. 1-15. Edited by W.T. Easterbrook and M.H. Watkins. Toronto: McClelland and Stewart, 1967.

Mallory, J.R.
Social Credit and the Federal Power in Canada. Social Credit in Alberta: Its Background and Development, 5. Toronto: University of Toronto Press, 1977. (First published 1954).

Martin, Chester
"Dominion Lands" Policy. The Carleton Library, no. 69. Toronto: McClelland and Stewart, 1973.

Masters, D.C.
Reciprocity, 1846-1911. Historical Booklet, no. 12. Ottawa: Canadian Historical Association, 1961.

The Reciprocity Treaty of 1854. The Carleton Library, no. 9. Toronto: McClelland and Stewart, 1963.

McDougall, Duncan M.
"Immigration Into Canada, 1851-1920." Canadian Journal of Economics and Political Science 27:2 (May 1961):162-175.

Meekison, J.P., ed.
Canadian Federalism: Myth or Reality. 2nd ed. Toronto: Methuen, 1971.

CONFEDERATION, NATIONAL POLICY, AND DOMINION-PROVINCIAL RELATIONS (cont'd)

Morton, W.L., ed.
Alexander Begg's Red River Journal and Other Papers Relative to the Red River Resistance of 1869-70. Champlain Society, publication no. 34. New York: Greenwood Press, 1969.

Ontario. Economic Council
Issues and Alternatives--1977: Intergovernmental Relations. Toronto: Queen's Printer, 1977.

Plumptre, A.F.W.
"The Nature of Political and Economic Development in the British Dominions." Canadian Journal of Economics and Political Science 3:4 (November 1937):489-507.

Porter, B., and Cuff, R., eds.
Enterprise and National Development: Essays in Canadian Business and Economic History. Toronto: Hakkert, 1973.

Robin, Martin
Canadian Provincial Politics: The Party Systems of the Ten Provinces. Scarborough, Ont.: Prentice-Hall, 1972.

Rowat, D., ed.
Provincial Government and Politics: Comparative Essays. Ottawa: Department of Political Science, Carleton University, 1972.

Ryerson, Stanley
Unequal Union: Confederation and the Roots of Conflict in the Canadas, 1815-1873. Toronto: Progress Books, 1968.

Saunders, S.A.
"The Reciprocity Treaty of 1854: A Regional Study." Canadian Journal of Economics and Political Science 2:1 (February 1936): 41-53.

Scheinberg, Stephen
"Invitation to Empire: Tariffs and American Economic Expansion in Canada." Business History Review 47:2 (Summer 1973):218-238.

Simeon, Richard
Federal-Provincial Diplomacy: The Making of Recent Policy in Canada. Studies in the Structure of Power. Toronto: University of Toronto Press, 1972.

Skelton, O.D., ed.
Life and Times of Sir Alexander Tilloch Galt. The Carleton Library, no. 26. Toronto: McClelland and Stewart, 1966.

Smiley, D.V., ed.
The Rowell-Sirois Report. The Carleton Library, no. 5. Toronto: McClelland and Stewart, 1964.

The Canadian Political Nationality. Toronto: Methuen, 1967.

Stanley, George F.G.
The Birth of Western Canada: A History of the Riel Rebellions. Toronto: University of Toronto Press, 1961. (First published 1936).

Taylor, K.W.
"Economic Implications of the Report of the Royal Commission on Price Spreads." Canadian Journal of Economics and Political Science 1 (August 1935).

Teeple, Gary
"Land, Labour and Capital in Pre-Confederation Canada." Capitalism and the National Question in Canada, pp. 43-66. Edited by G. Teeple. Toronto: University of Toronto Press, 1972.

Timlin, Mabel
"Canada's Immigration Policy, 1896-1910." Canadian Journal of Economics and Political Science 26:4 (November 1960):517-532.

Tucker, Gilbert N.
The Canadian Commercial Revolution, 1845-1851. The Carleton Library, no. 19. Toronto: McClelland and Stewart, 1964.

Underhill, Frank
"Some Aspects of Upper Canadian Radical Opinion in the Decade Before Confederation." In Search of Canadian Liberalism, pp. 43-67. Toronto: Macmillan, 1960.

The Image of Confederation. The Massey Lectures, 3rd series. Toronto: CBC Publications, 1964.

Woodsworth, J.S.
My Neighbour: A Study of City Conditions, a Plea for Social Service. The Social History of Canada. Toronto: University of Toronto Press, 1972. (First published 1911).

4. CITY POLITICS

Ames, H.B.
City Below the Hill: A Sociological Study of a Portion of the City of Montreal, Canada. The Social History of Canada. Toronto: University of Toronto Press, 1972. (First published 1897).

Artibise, Alan F.J.
Winnipeg: A Social History of Urban Growth, 1874-1914. Montreal: McGill-Queen's University Press, 1975.

Axworthy, L., and Gillies, J.M., eds.
The City: Canada's Prospects, Canada's Problems. Toronto: Butterworth, 1973.

Barker, G.; Penny, J.; and Seccombe, W.
Highrise and Superprofits. Kitchener: Dumont Press Graphix, 1973.

Blumenfeld, H.
The Modern Metropolis. Montreal: Harvest House, 1971.

Bryant, R.W.G.
Land: Private Property, Public Control. Montreal: Harvest House, 1972.

Budden, S., and Ernst, J.
The Movable Airport: The Politics of Government Planning. Toronto: Hakkert, 1973.

Carver, H.
Cities in the Suburbs. Toronto: University of Toronto Press, 1962.

Compassionate Landscape: Places and People in a Man's Life. Toronto: University of Toronto Press, 1975.

Caulfield, Jon
The Tiny Perfect Mayor. Toronto: James Lorimer, 1974.

Clairmont, Donald H., and Magill, Dennis W.
Africville: The Life and Death of a Canadian Black Community. Toronto: McClelland and Stewart, 1974.

Dennis, M., and Fish, S.
Programs In Search of a Policy: Low Income Housing in Canada. Toronto: Hakkert, 1972.

Fraser, Graham
Fighting Back: Urban Renewal in Trefann Court. Toronto: Hakkert, 1972.

CITY POLITICS (cont'd)

Garner, Hugh
Cabbagetown. Toronto: Ryerson Press, 1968. (First published 1950).

Gertler, L., ed.
Planning the Canadian Environment. Montreal: Harvest House, 1968.

Granatstein, J.L.
Marlborough Marathon: One Street Against a Developer. Toronto: Hakkert, 1971.

Gutstein, Donald
Vancouver Ltd. Toronto: James Lorimer, 1975.

Haworth, L.
The Good City. Bloomington: Indiana University Press, 1963.

Hugo-Brunt, M.
The History of City Planning; A Survey. Environment series. Montreal: Harvest House, 1972.

Katz, Michael
"The People of a Canadian City, 1851-2." Canadian Historical Review 53:4 (December 1972):402-426.

Keating, D.R.
The Power to Make It Happen: Mass-Based Community Organizing; What It Is and How It Works. Toronto: Green Tree, 1975.

Lithwick, N.H.
Urban Canada: Problems and Prospects; A Report. Ottawa: CMHC, 1970.

Lorimer, James
The Real World of City Politics. Toronto: James, Lewis and Samuel, 1970.

Citizen's Guide to City Politics. Toronto: James Lorimer, 1972.

Lorimer, James, and Phillips, Myfanwy
Working People: Life in a Downtown City Neighbourhood. Toronto: James, Lewis and Samuel, 1971.

Lorimer, James, and Ross, Evelyn, eds.
The Second City Book: The Planning and Politics of Canada's Cities. Toronto: James Lorimer, 1977.

CITY POLITICS (cont'd)

Parnell, M.
Rape of the Block. Edmonton: Edmonton Social Planning Council, 1972.

Pasternak, J.
The Kitchener Market Fight. Toronto: Hakkert, 1975.

Powell, A., ed.
The City: Attacking Modern Myths. Toronto: McClelland and Stewart, 1972.

Richardson, B.
The Future of Canadian Cities. Toronto: New Press, 1972.

Rutherford, P.
Saving the Canadian City, the First Phase 1880-1920: An Anthology of Articles on Urban Reform. Toronto: University of Toronto Press, 1974.

Schwilgin, F.A.
Town Planning Guidelines. Ottawa: Department of Public Works, 1973.

Seeley, John R., et al.
Crestwood Heights: A Study of the Culture of Suburban Life. Toronto: University of Toronto Press, 1956.

Sewell, J.
Up Against City Hall. Toronto: James Lorimer, 1972.

Stein, D.L.
Toronto For Sale: The Destruction of a City. Toronto: New Press, 1972.

Stetler, Gilbert A., and Artibise, Alan F.J., eds.
The Canadian City: Essays in Urban History. The Carleton Library, no. 109. Toronto: McClelland and Stewart, 1977.

VI. CULTURE AND NATIONALISM

Acorn, Milton
I've Tasted My Blood: Poems 1956-1968. Toronto: Ryerson, 1969.

More Poems for People. Toronto: NC Press, 1972.

Atwood, Margaret
Survival: A Thematic Guide to Canadian Literature. Toronto: Anansi, 1972.

Surfacing. Toronto: McClelland and Stewart, 1972.

Bailey, Alfred Goldsworthy
Culture and Nationality: Essays by A.G. Bailey. The Carleton Library, no. 58. Toronto: McClelland and Stewart, 1972.

Barker, G; Lévesque, A.; Dozois, G.; and Vachon, G.A.
"Les Idées Politiques des Canadiens-Français: Four Nationalist Movements." Study for the Royal Commission on Bilingualism and Biculturalism. Ottawa: Queen's Printer, 1968.

Bell, David
"The Loyalist Tradition in Canada." Journal of Canadian Studies 5:2 (May 1970):22-33.

Berger, Carl
The Sense of Power: Studies in the Ideas of Canadian Imperialism, 1867-1914. Toronto: University of Toronto Press, 1970.

The Writing of Canadian History. Toronto: Oxford University Press, 1976.

Cairns, Alan C.
"Political Science in Canada and the Americanization Issue." Canadian Journal of Political Science 8:2 (June 1975):191-234.

Canada. Royal Commission on National Development in the Arts, Letters and Sciences
The Massey Report. Ottawa: King's Printer, 1951.

Canada. Royal Commission on Publications
The O'Leary Report. Ottawa: Queen's Printer, 1961.

Canada. Senate Report
"The Uncertain Mirror." Report of the Special Senate Committee on Mass Media. Ottawa: Information Canada, 1970.

Words, Music, and Dollars: A Study of the Economics of Publishing and Broadcasting. Report of the Special Senate Committee on Mass Media. Ottawa: Information Canada, 1970.

CULTURE AND NATIONALISM (cont'd)

Canadian Dimension
"The NDP and the Waffle." (Special Supplement) 1:8 (April 1971).

Cappon, Paul, ed.
In Our Own House: Social Perspectives on Canadian Literature. Toronto: McClelland and Stewart, 1978.

Carr, D.W.
Recovering Canada's Nationhood. Ottawa: Canada Publishing, 1971.

Cook, Ramsay
Canada and the French-Canadian Question. Toronto: Macmillan, 1966.

Cook, Ramsay, ed.
French-Canadian Nationalism: An Anthology. Toronto: Macmillan, 1969.

Crean, Susan M.
Who's Afraid of Canadian Culture? Don Mills, Ont.: General Publishing, 1976.

Dexter, Gail
"Yes, Cultural Imperialism Too!" Close the 49th Parallel Etc.: The Americanization of Canada, pp. 157-167. Edited by Ian Lumsden. Toronto: University of Toronto Press, 1970.

Drache, Daniel
"The Canadian Bourgeoisie and Its National Consciousness." Close the 49th Parallel Etc.: The Americanization of Canada, pp. 3-25. Edited by Ian Lumsden. Toronto: University of Toronto Press, 1970.

"Ten Good Years: The Beginnings of Hinterland Resistance." This Magazine 8:3 (August-September 1974):30-34.

"Going Down the Nationalist Road...Slowly." This Magazine 7:2 (August 1973):28-30.

"Walter Gordon: Going Down Without the Ship." This Magazine 10:3 (June-July 1976):3-7.

Frye, Northrop
The Bush Garden: Essays on the Canadian Imagination. Toronto: Anansi, 1971.

Gagne, Wallace, ed.
Nationalism, Technology and the Future of Canada. Toronto: Macmillan, 1976.

CULTURE AND NATIONALISM (cont'd)

Godfrey, David, and Watkins, Mel
Gordon to Watkins to You. A Documentary: The Battle for Control of Our Economy. Toronto: New Press, 1970.

Gonick, Cy, and Finnigan, B., eds.
Making It: The Canadian Dream. Toronto: McClelland and Stewart, 1972.

Gordon, Walter L.
Troubled Canada: The Need for New Domestic Policies. Toronto: McClelland and Stewart, 1961.

A Choice for Canada: Independent or Colonial Status. Toronto: McClelland and Stewart, 1966.

Storm Signals: New Economic Policies for Canada. Toronto: McClelland and Stewart, 1975.

Grant, George
Lament for a Nation: The Defeat of Canadian Nationalism. Canada Today. Toronto: McClelland and Stewart, 1967.

Gruneau, Rick, and Albinson, John, eds.
Canadian Sport: Sociological Perspectives. Don Mills, Ont.: Addison-Wesley, 1976.

Hardin, Herschel
A Nation Unaware: The Canadian Economic Culture. Vancouver: J.J. Douglas, 1974.

Hodgetts, A.B.
What Culture? What Heritage? A Study of Civic Education in Canada. Curriculum series, 5. Toronto: Ontario Institute for Studies in Education, 1968.

Horowitz, Gad
"Conservativism, Liberalism, and Socialism in Canada: An Interpretation." Canada: A Sociological Profile, 2nd ed., pp. 8-23. Edited by W.E. Mann. Toronto: Copp Clark, 1971. Original in Canadian Journal of Economics and Political Science 32:2 (May 1966):143-171.

Johnson, Harry G.
The Canadian Quandary. Toronto: McClelland and Stewart, 1977.

"Problems of Canadian Nationalism." The Canadian Quandary, pp. 11-21. Toronto: McClelland and Stewart, 1977.

Johnstone, John C.
"Definitions of Canadian Society." The Canadian Political Process: A Reader, pp. 94-131. Edited by O.M. Kruhlack. Toronto: Holt, Rinehart and Winston, 1970.

Kierans, Eric
"Canadian Resources Policy." Canadian Forum 52 (June-July 1973): 56-63.

Laxer, James
"The Americanization of the Canadian Student Movement." Close the 49th Parallel Etc.: The Americanization of Canada, pp. 275-286. Edited by Ian Lumsden. Toronto: University of Toronto Press, 1970.

Laxer, James, and Laxer, Robert
The Liberal Idea of Canada. Toronto: James Lorimer, 1977.

Laxer, Robert
Canada's Unions. Toronto: James Lorimer, 1976.

Lee, Dennis
"Writing in Colonial Space." Open Letter, Second Series, 6 (Fall 1973).

Levitt, Kari
"Decolonizing Canada and Quebec." Canadian Forum 51 (March 1972).

Lind, Loren
"New Canadianism: Melting the Ethnics in Toronto Schools." The Politics of the Canadian Public School, pp. 103-117. Edited by G. Martell. Toronto: James Lorimer, 1974.

Lorimer, James
"The Political Economy of Canadian Publishing." This Magazine 9:3 (July-August 1975):22-28.

Lumsden, Ian, ed.
Close the 49th Parallel, Etc.: The Americanization of Canada. Toronto: University of Toronto Press, 1970.

Macpherson, C.B.
"After Strange Gods: Canadian Political Science 1973." Perspectives on the Social Sciences in Canada, pp. 52-76. Edited by T.N. Guinsberg and Grant Reuber. Toronto: University of Toronto Press, 1974.

Marchak, M. Patricia
Ideological Perspectives on Canada. Series in Canadian Sociology. Toronto: McGraw-Hill Ryerson, 1975.

CULTURE AND NATIONALISM (cont'd)

Mathews, Robin, and Steele, James, eds.
The Struggle for Canadian Universities: A Dossier. Toronto: Toronto: New Press, 1969.

Mathews, Robin
"Canadian Culture and the Liberal Ideology." Canada Ltd.: The Political Economy of Dependency, pp. 213-231. Edited by Robert Laxer. Toronto: McClelland and Stewart, 1973.

"Facing Up to a U.S. Military Occupation of Canada: Three Recent Political Novels." This Magazine 8:2 (June 1974):24-28.

"Canadian Literature: The Necessary Revolution." The Politics of the Canadian Public School, pp. 134-148. Edited by G. Martell. Toronto: James Lorimer, 1974.

The Language of Fire: Poems of Love and Struggle. Toronto: Steel Rail Press, 1976.

Canadian Literature. Toronto: Steel Rail Press, 1978.

Moore, Steve, and Wells, Debbi
Imperialism and the National Question in Canada. Toronto: New Hogtown Press, 1975.

Neatby, Hilda
So Little For the Mind. 2nd ed. Toronto: Clarke Irwin, 1953.

Ontario. Royal Commission on Book Publishing
Canadian Publishers and Canadian Publishing. Ottawa: Queen's Printer, 1971.

Peers, Frank
The Politics of Canadian Broadcasting, 1920-1951. Toronto: University of Toronto Press, 1969.

Prang, Margaret
"The Origins of Public Broadcasting in Canada." Canadian Historical Review 46:1 (March 1965):1-31.

Repo, Satu
"From Pilgrim's Progress to Sesame Street: 125 Years of Colonial Readers." This Magazine 7:2 (August 1973):11-15.

"The American Comic Book: Proletarian Literature for Children." This Magazine 8:1 (March 1974):8-11.

Resnick, Philip
The Land of Cain: Class and Nationalism in English Canada 1945-1975. Vancouver: New Star Books, 1977.

CULTURE AND NATIONALISM (cont'd)

Rosenblum, Simon
"Economic Nationalism and the English-Canadian Socialist Mind." Our Generation 11:1 (Fall 1975):5-15.

Rotstein, Abraham
The Precarious Homestead: Essays on Economics, Technology and Nationalism. Toronto: New Press, 1973.

"Canada: The New Nationalism." Foreign Affairs 55:1 (October 1976): 97-118.

"The World Upside Down." Canadian Journal of Political and Social Theory 2:2 (Spring-Summer 1978):5-30.

Rotstein, Abraham, and Lax, Gary, eds.
Independence: The Canadian Challenge. Toronto: Committee For An Independent Canada, 1972.

Getting It Back: A Program for Canadian Independence. Toronto: Clarke Irwin, 1974.

Russell, Peter, ed.
Nationalism in Canada. Toronto: McGraw-Hill, 1966.

Salutin, Rick
"The State or the States: On the CBC." This Magazine 7:3 (November 1973):12-16.

Saul, J., and Heron, Craig, eds.
Imperialism, Nationalism and Canada. Toronto: New Hogtown Press, 1977.

Smith, Denis
Gentle Patriot: A Political Biography of Walter Gordon. Edmonton: Hurtig Publishers, 1973.

Smollett, Eleanor
"Schools and the Illusion of Choice: The Middle Class, and the 'Open' Classroom." The Politics of the Canadian Public School, pp. 92-102. Edited by G. Martell. Toronto: James Lorimer, 1974.

Steele, James, and Mathews, Robin
"The Universities: Takeover of the Mind." Close the 49th Parallel, Etc.: The Americanization of Canada, pp. 169-178. Edited by Ian Lumsden. Toronto: University of Toronto Press, 1970.

Sullivan, John
"A Year of the New Maclean's: Import-Substitution in the Ideology Market." This Magazine 11:1 (January-February 1977):5-9.

Sutherland, John
Essays, Controversies and Poems. New Canadian Library Original. Edited by Miriam Waddington. Toronto: McClelland and Stewart, 1972.

Symons, T.H.B.
To Know Ourselves: The Report of the Commission on Canadian Studies. 2 vols. Ottawa: AUCC, 1976. Also The Symons Report. 1 vol. abridged. Toronto: McClelland and Stewart, 1977.

Taylor, Charles
"Nationalism and the Political Intelligentsia." Queen's Quarterly 72 (Spring 1965).

Teeple, Gary, ed.
Capitalism and the National Question in Canada. Toronto: University of Toronto Press, 1972.

Vallieres, Pierre
White Niggers of America. Toronto: McClelland and Stewart, 1971.

Warnock, Jack
"Imperialism and the Canadian Left." Canadian Dimension 11:4 (March 1975).

"All the News It Pays to Print." Close the 49th Parallel, Etc.: The Americanization of Canada, pp. 117-134. Edited by Ian Lumsden. Toronto: University of Toronto Press, 1970.

Watkins, Mel
"Contradictions and Alternatives in Canada's Future." Canada Ltd.: The Political Economy of Dependency, pp. 250-269. Edited by Robert Laxer. Toronto: McClelland and Stewart, 1973.

Wolfe, Morris
"Empire in Print: Maclean-Hunter." Canadian Forum 53 (September 1973).

Wright, Judy, and Magidson, Debbie
"Making Films For Your Own People." This Magazine 8:4 (November-December 1974):21-27.

VII. WOMEN

Acton, Janice, et al., eds.
Women at Work: Ontario 1850-1930. Toronto: Canadian Women's Educational Press, 1974.

Allingham, John D.
The Demographic Background to Change in the Number and Composition of Female Wage-Earners in Canada, 1951 to 1961. Ottawa: Dominion Bureau of Statistics, 1967.

Ambert, Anne-Marie
Sex Structure. Rev. ed. New York: Longmans, 1977.

Andrews, Margaret
"Attitudes in Canadian Women's History, 1945-1975." Journal of Canadian Studies 12:4 (Summer 1977):69-78.

Armstrong, Hugh, and Armstrong, Pat
"The Segregated Participation of Women in the Canadian Labour Force, 1941-71." Canadian Review of Sociology and Anthropology 12:4 (November 1975):370-384.

The Double Ghetto. Toronto: McClelland and Stewart, 1978.

Bennett, James E., and Loewe, Pierre M.
Women in Business: A Shocking Waste of Human Resources. A Financial Post Book. Toronto: Maclean-Hunter, 1975.

Bohnen, Linda A.
"Women Workers in Ontario: A Socio-Legal History." University of Toronto Faculty of Law Review 1974.

Canada. Royal Commission on the Status of Women
Report. Ottawa: Information Canada, 1970.

Carson, John J.
"Sex and the Public Service." Canadian Personnel and Industrial Relations Journal 17:2 (March 1970):13-17.

Cheda, Sherrill
"Indian Women: A Historical Example and a Contemporary View." Women in Canada, rev. ed., pp. 195-208. Edited by Marylee Stephenson. Don Mills, Ont.: General Publishing, 1977. (First edition 1973).

Clark, Melissa
"The Status of Women in Relation to Transitions in the Mode of Production." The Occasional Papers of the McMaster University Sociology of Women Programme 1 (Spring 1977):128-164.

WOMEN (cont'd)

Cleverdon, Catherine Lyle
The Woman Suffrage Movement in Canada. 2nd ed. The Social History of Canada, 18. Toronto: University of Toronto Press, 1974. (First edition 1950).

Coburn, Judi
"'I See and Am Silent': A Short History of Nursing in Ontario." Women At Work: Ontario 1850-1930, pp. 125-138. Edited by Janice Acton, et al. Toronto: Canadian Women's Educational Press, 1974.

Cook, Ramsay, and Mitchenson, Wendy, eds.
The Proper Sphere: Woman's Place in Canadian Society. Toronto: Oxford University Press, 1976.

Cruikshank, Julie
"Matrifocal Families in the Canadian North." The Canadian Family. A Book of Readings. Edited by K. Ishwaran. Toronto: Holt, Rinehart and Winston, 1971.

Duffy, Ann
"Women Outside the Labour Force." The Occasional Papers of the McMaster University Sociology of Women Programme 1 (Spring 1977): 1-31.

Eichler, Margrit
"Women as Personal Dependents: A Critique of Theories of the Stratification of the Sexes and an Alternative Approach." Women in Canada, rev. ed., pp. 49-69. Edited by Marylee Stephenson. Don Mills, Ont.: General Publishing, 1977. (First edition 1973).

Eichler, Margrit; Newton, Jennifer; and Primrose, Lynne
"A Bibliography of Materials on Canadian Women." Women in Canada, rev. ed., pp. 275-360. Edited by Marylee Stephenson. Don Mills, Ont.: General Publishing, 1977. (First edition 1973).

Gelber, Sylvia
"Which Side Are You On?" Canadian Labour 17:5 (May 1972):4-6.

Graham, Elizabeth
"Schoolmarms and Early Teaching in Ontario." Women at Work: Ontario 1850-1930, pp. 165-209. Edited by Janice Acton, et al. Toronto: Canadian Women's Educational Press, 1974.

Hill, Christina Maria
"Women in the Canadian Economy." Canada Ltd.: The Political Economy of Dependence, pp. 84-106. Edited by Robert Laxer. Toronto: McClelland and Stewart, 1973.

WOMEN (cont'd)

Innis, Mary Quayle, ed.
The Clear Spirit: Twenty Canadian Women and Their Times. Toronto: University of Toronto Press, 1966.

James, Alice
"Poverty: Canada's Legacy to Women." *Women Unite! An Anthology of the Canadian Women's Movement*, pp. 125-138. Toronto: Canadian Women's Educational Press, 1972.

Jewett, Pauline
"The Working Woman." *Continuous Learning* 4:5 (September-October 1965):216-220.

Johnson, Leo
"The Political Economy of Ontario Women in the Nineteenth Century." *Women at Work: Ontario 1850-1930*, pp. 13-31. Edited by Janice Acton, et al. Toronto: Canadian Women's Educational Press, 1974.

Kidd, Dorothy
"Women's Organization: Learning from Yesterday." *Women at Work: Ontario 1850-1930*, pp. 331-361. Edited by Janice Acton, et al. Toronto: Canadian Women's Educational Press, 1974.

Klein, Alice, and Roberts, Wayne
"Beseiged Innocence: The "Problem" and Problems of Working Women --Toronto, 1896-1914." *Women at Work: Ontario 1850-1930*, pp. 211 -259. Edited by Janice Acton, et al. Toronto: Canadian Women's Educational Press, 1974.

Lang, Lynn
"Women on Welfare." *Women Unite! An Anthology of the Canadian Women's Movement*, pp. 152-157. Toronto: Canadian Women's Educational Press, 1972.

Leslie, Genevieve
"Domestic Service in Canada, 1880-1920." *Women at Work: Ontario 1850-1930*, pp. 71-125. Edited by Janice Acton, et al. Toronto: Canadian Women's Educational Press, 1974.

Macleod, Catherine
"Women in Production: The Toronto Dressmakers' Strike of 1931." *Women at Work: Ontario 1850-1930*, pp. 309-329. Edited by Janice Acton, et al. Toronto: Canadian Women's Educational Press, 1974.

Manitouwabi, Edna
"An Ojibwa Girl in the City." *This Magazine is About Schools* 4:4 (Fall 1970).

Marchak, M. Patricia
"The Canadian Labour Farce: Jobs for Women." *Women in Canada*, rev. ed., pp. 148-159. Edited by Marylee Stephenson. Don Mills, Ont.: General Publishing, 1977. (First edition 1973).

WOMEN (cont'd)

Matheson, Gwen, ed.
Women in the Canadian Mosaic. Toronto: Peter Martin Associates, 1976.

Mathews, Ann Martin
"The Case of the Migrant Wife: Looking at the World From the Underdog Perspective." The Occasional Papers of the McMaster University Sociology of Women Programme 1 (Spring 1977):165-194.

McClung, Nellie
In Times Like These. Edited by V. Strong-Boag. The Social History of Canada. Toronto: University of Toronto Press, 1972. (First published 1915).

McDonald, Lynn
"Wages of Work: A Widening Gap Between Women and Men." Women in Canada, rev. ed, pp. 181-191. Edited by Marylee Stephenson. Don Mills, Ont.: General Publishing, 1977. (First edition 1973).

McFarland, Joan
"Economics and Women: A Critique of the Scope of Traditional Analysis and Research." Atlantis 1:2 (Spring 1976):26-41.

Meissner, Martin; Humphreys, Elizabeth W.; Meis, Scott M.; and Scheu, William J.
"No Exit for Wives: Sexual Division of Labour and the Cumulation of Household Demands." Canadian Review of Sociology and Anthropology 12:4 (November 1975):424-439.

Menzies, J.
"Votes for Saskatchewan Women." Politics in Saskatchewan. Edited by Norman Ward and Duff Spafford. Toronto: Longmans, 1969.

Morton, Peggy
"Women's Work is Never Done...Or the Production, Maintenance and Reproduction of Labour Power." Women Unite! An Anthology of the Canadian Women's Movement, pp. 46-68. Toronto: Canadian Women's Educational Press, 1972.

Nunes, Maxine, and White, Deanna
The Lace Ghetto. New Woman series, 3. Toronto: New Press, 1972.

Pierson, Ruth
"Women's Emancipation and the Recruitment of Women into the Labour Force in World War II." The Neglected Majority: Essays in Canadian Women's History, pp. 125-145. Edited by S. Trofimenkoff and A. Prentice. Toronto: McClelland and Stewart, 1977.

Ramkhalawansingh, Ceta
"Women During the Great War." Women at Work: Ontario 1850-1930, pp. 261-307. Edited by Janice Acton, et al. Toronto: Canadian Women's Educational Press, 1974.

Ritchie, Laurell
"'Affirmative Action': What Women Stand to Lose." This Magazine 10:1 (February-March 1976):25-27.

Roberts, Wayne
Honest Womanhood: Feminism, Femininity and Class Consciousness Among Toronto Working Women, 1893 to 1914. Toronto: New Hogtown Press, 1976.

Rosenbluth, Vera
"Women in Prison." Women in Canada, rev. ed., pp. 209-227. Edited by Marylee Stephenson. Don Mills, Ont.: General Publishing, 1977. (First edition 1973).

Rotenberg, Lori
"The Wayward Worker: Toronto's Prostitute at the Turn of the Century." Women at Work: Ontario 1850-1930, pp. 33-69. Edited by Janice Acton, et al. Toronto: Canadian Women's Educational Press, 1974.

Rowntree, Mickey, and Rowntree, John
More on the Political Economy of Women's Liberation. Toronto: New Hogtown Press, 1973.

Saunders, Eileen
"Implications of the Domestic Role of Women." Alternate Routes 1 (1977):142-157.

Schmid, Carol
"Sex Antagonism: Toward an Understanding of the Sex-Caste Analogy and Its Application to Women in the Labour Force." The Occasional Papers of the McMaster University Sociology of Women Programme 1 (Spring 1977):110-127.

"The 'Changing' Status of Women in the United States and Canada." The Occasional Papers of the McMaster University Sociology of Women Programme 1 (Spring 1977):231-266.

Smith, Dorothy E.
"Women, the Family and Corporate Capitalism." Women in Canada, rev. ed., pp. 14-48. Edited by Marylee Stephenson. Don Mills, Ont.: General Publishing, 1977. (First edition 1973).

WOMEN (cont'd)

Stephenson, Marylee
"Housewives in Women's Liberation: Social Change as Role-Making." Women in Canada, rev. ed., pp. 109-125. Edited by Marylee Stephenson. Don Mills, Ont.: General Publishing, 1977. (First edition 1973).

Stephenson, Marylee, ed.
Women in Canada. Rev. ed. Don Mills, Ont.: General Publishing, 1977. (First edition 1973).

Stoddart, Jennifer
"The Woman Suffrage Bill in Quebec: Public Opinion as Reflected in the Press." Women in Canada, pp. 90-106. Edited by Marylee Stephenson. Toronto: New Press, 1973.

Strong-Boag, Veronica, ed.
In Times Like These by Nellie McClung. The Social History of Canada. Toronto: University of Toronto Press, 1972. (First published 1915).

"Cousin Cinderella: A Guide to Historical Literature Pertaining to Canadian Women." Women in Canada, rev. ed., pp. 245-274. Edited by Marylee Stephenson. Don Mills, Ont.: General Publishing, 1977. (First edition 1973).

The Parliament of Women. Ottawa: National Museum, 1976.

Trofimenkoff, Susan, and Prentice, Alison, ed.
The Neglected Majority: Essays in Canadian Women's History. Toronto: McClelland and Stewart, 1977.

Ursel, Jane
"Sexism, Sexual Repression and Social Control." The Occasional Papers of the McMaster University Sociology of Women Programme 1 (Spring 1977):319-342.

Van Stolk, Mary
Man and Woman. Toronto: McClelland and Stewart, 1968.

VIII. QUEBEC

Armstrong, Elizabeth
Crisis in Quebec, 1914-18. The Carleton Library, no. 74. Toronto: McClelland and Stewart, 1974. (First published 1937).

Armstrong, Jill
"Canadians in Crisis: The Nature and Source of Support for Leadership in a National Emergency." Canadian Review of Sociology and Anthropology 9:4 (November 1973):299-324.

Arnaud, Nicole, and Dofny, Jacques
Nationalism and the National Question. Montreal: Black Rose Books, 1977.

Audet, Louis-Philippe
Histoire de l'enseignement au Québec. Montreal: Holt, Rinehart and Winston, 1971.

Auf der Maur, Nick
"Power Corrupts, Absolutely." Last Post 2:3 (December-January 1971-72):14-18.

"The Trigger was the 'La Presse' Affair." Last Post 2:3 (December-January 1971-72):8-13.

"The May Revolt Shakes Quebec." Last Post 2:6 (July 1972):10-25.

Barker, G.; Lévesque, A.; Dozois, G.; and Vachon, G.A.
"Les idées politiques des canadiens-français--Four Nationalist Movements." Study for the Royal Commission on Bilingualism and Biculturalism. Ottawa: Information Canada, 1968.

Beattie, Christopher
Minority Men in a Majority Setting: Middle-Level Francophones in the Canadian Public Service. The Carleton Library, no. 92. Toronto: McClelland and Stewart, 1975.

Bergeron, Leandre
The History of Quebec: A Patriote's Handbook. Rev. ed. Toronto: NC Press, 1971.

Bernier, Bernard
"The Penetration of Capitalism in Quebec Agriculture." Canadian Review of Sociology and Anthropology 13:4 (November 1976):422-434.

Black, Conrad
Duplessis. Toronto: McClelland and Stewart, 1976.

QUEBEC (cont'd)

Bourque, Gilles
Classes sociales et question nationale au Québec (1760-1840). Collection aspects, 7. Montréal: Parti Pris, 1970.

"La nation." Les Cahiers du Socialisme 1 (1978):187-197.

Bourque, Gilles, and Laurin-Frenette, Nicole
"Social Classes and Nationalist Ideologies in Quebec, 1760-1970." Capitalism and the National Question in Canada, pp. 185-210. Edited by G. Teeple. Toronto: University of Toronto Press, 1972.

Brazeau, Jacques
"Quebec's Emerging Middle Class." French Canadian Society, pp. 319-327. Edited by Marcel Rioux and Yves Martin. Toronto: McClelland and Stewart, 1964.

Brunelle, Dorval
"L'intervention de l'état dans l'économie et la question du rapport entre le fédéral et les provinces." Les Cahiers du Socialisme 1 (1978):51-86.

Brunet, Michel
"The British Conquest: Canadian Social Scientists and the Fate of the Canadiens." Canadian Historical Review 40:2 (June 1959): 93-107.

Bureau de la Statistique du Québec
Les tendances de l'emploi par secteurs d'activité au Québec. Québec: Ministère du Travail et de la Main d'oeuvre, 1961-70.

Géographie de l'industrie manufacturière du Québec. Québec: Ministère de l'Industrie et du Commerce, 1970.

Cahiers de l'Université du Québec
Economie Québécoise. Montréal: Les Presses de l'Université du Québec, 1970.

Caloren, Fred
"The War Measures Act and the Politics of Functionalism." Our Generation 7:3 (October-November 1970):21-33.

Canada. Royal Commission on Bilingualism and Biculturalism
Report. 3 vols. Ottawa: Information Canada, 1969.

Canadian Forum
"Quebec Planning for Independence." 56:668 (February 1977).

Chodos, R., and Auf der Maur, N.
Quebec: A Chronicle 1968-1972. Toronto: James Lorimer, 1972.

QUEBEC (cont'd)

Collectif d'auteurs
Les travailleurs québécois, 1851-1896. Montréal: Les Presses de l'Université du Québec, 1973.

Cook, Ramsay
Canada and the French-Canadian Question. Toronto: Macmillan, 1966.

Cook, Ramsay, ed.
French-Canadian Nationalism: An Anthology. Toronto: Macmillan, 1969.

Craig, Gerald M., ed.
Lord Durham's Report. The Carleton Library, no. 1. Toronto: McClelland and Stewart, 1963.

Creighton, Donald
"The Myth of Biculturalism." Towards the Discovery of Canada, pp. 256-270. Toronto: Macmillan, 1972.

Cuneo, Carl J., and Curtis, James E.
"Quebec Separatism: An Analysis of Determinants Within Social-Class Levels." Canadian Review of Sociology and Anthropology 11:1 (February 1974):1-29.

Dion, Gérard
"The Trade Union Movement in Quebec." University of Toronto Quarterly 27 (April 1958).

Dion, Leon
La prochaine révolution. Montréal: Leméac, 1973. English edition: Quebec: The Unfinished Revolution. Montreal: McGill-Queen's University Press, 1976.

"Towards a Self-Determined Consciousness." Quebec Society and Politics: Views from the Inside, pp. 26-38. Edited by D.C. Thomson. Toronto: McClelland and Stewart, 1973.

"Quebec and the Future of Canada." Quebec Society and Politics: Views from the Inside, pp. 251-262. Edited by D.C. Thomson. Toronto: McClelland and Stewart, 1973.

Drache, Daniel, ed.
Quebec--Only the Beginning: The Manifestoes of the Common Front. Toronto: New Press, 1972.

Dumas, Evelyn
The Bitter Thirties in Quebec. Montreal: Black Rose Books, 1975.

QUEBEC (cont'd)

Dumont, Fernand, and Montminy, Jean-Paul, éds.
Le pouvoir dans la société canadienne-française. Québec: Les Presses de l'Université Laval, 1966.

Escande, C.
Les classes sociales au CEGEP. Collection aspects, no. 21. Montréal: Parti Pris, 1973.

Faucher, A., and Lamontagne, M.
"History of Industrial Development." French Canadian Society, vol. I, pp. 257-271. Edited by M. Rioux and Y. Martin. Toronto: McClelland and Stewart, 1964.

Faucher, Albert
Québec en Amérique au XIXe siècle. Histoire économique et sociale du Canada français. Montréal: Fides, 1973.

Fortin, Gerald
"Le nationalisme canadien-française et les classes sociales." Revue d'histoire de l'Amérique français 22:4 (March 1969): 525-535.

Fournier, Pierre
The Quebec Establishment: The Ruling Class and the State. Montreal: Black Rose Books, 1976.

Gagnon, Charles
"Classe et conscience de classe." Socialisme 69:18 (July-September 1969):66-74.

Gagnon, Lebel
Droit du travail en vigueur au Québec. Québec: Les Presses de l'Université Laval, 1971.

Gagnon, Lysiane
"Les Conclusions de Rapport B.B.: De Durham à Laurendeau-Dunton: Variations sur le thème de la dualité canadienne." Economie Québécoise, pp. 233-252. Montréal: Les Presses de l'Université du Québec, 1969.

"The Common Front and Quebec Teachers." The Politics of the Canadian Public School, pp. 165-171. Edited by G. Martell. Toronto: James Lorimer, 1974.

Glenday, Dan
"The Dominion Government as Gatekeeper to the Canadian Mosaic." Alternate Routes 1 (1977):38-57.

QUEBEC (cont'd)

Granatstein, J.L., and Hitsman, J.M.
Broken Promises: A History of Conscription in Canada. Toronto: Oxford University Press, 1977.

Groupe de recherches économiques
Coopératives de production, usines populaires et pouvoir ouvrier. Montréal: Editions Québécoises, 1973.

Guindon, Hubert
"Social Unrest, Social Class and Quebec's Bureaucratic Revolution." *Queen's Quarterly* 71:2 (1964).

"Two Cultures: An Essay on Nationalism, Class, and Ethnic Tension." *Contemporary Canada*, pp. 33-59. Edited by Richard H. Leach. Toronto: University of Toronto Press, 1968.

"The Modernization of Quebec and the Legitimacy of the Feudal State." *Modernization and the Canadian State*, pp. 212-246. Edited by D. Glenday, A. Turowetz, and H. Guindon. Toronto: Macmillan, 1977.

Haggart, Ron, and Golden, Aubrey E.
Rumours of War. Toronto: New Press, 1971.

Halary, Charles, et Mascotto, Jacques
"Dialectique matérialiste et nationalisme historique." *Les Cahiers du Socialisme* 1 (1978):87-186.

Harvey, F., éd.
Aspects historiques du mouvement ouvrier au Québec. Montréal: Editions du Boréal Express, 1973.

Hughes, E.C.
French Canada in Transition. Chicago: University of Chicago Press, 1963. (First published 1943).

Hughes, E.C., and McDonald, M.L.
"French and English in the Economic Structure of Montreal." *Canadian Journal of Economics and Political Science* 7:4 (November 1941):493-505.

Johnson, Daniel
Egalité ou indépendance. Montréal: Editions Renaissance, 1965.

Jones, Richard
Community in Crisis: French-Canadian Nationalism in Perspective. The Carleton Library, no. 59. Toronto: McClelland and Stewart, 1972.

Joy, Richard J.
Languages in Conflict: The Canadian Experience. The Carleton Library, no. 61. Toronto: McClelland and Stewart, 1972.

QUEBEC (cont'd)

Kwavnick, David, ed.
The Tremblay Report: Report of the Royal Commission of Inquiry on Constitutional Problems. The Carleton Library, no. 64. Toronto: McClelland and Stewart, 1973.

Lapalme, Georges-Emile
Le paradis du pouvoir. Collection vies et mémoires. Montréal: Leméac, 1973.

Last Post
"No Minority Group Is Treated Better." 2:3 (December-January 1971-72):24-25.

Latouche, Daniel
"La vrai nature de...la révolution tranquille." Canadian Journal of Political Science 7:3 (September 1974):525-536.

Laurendeau, André
Witness for Quebec. Toronto: Macmillan, 1973.

Laxer, James
"Quebec in the Canadian Federal State." Canada Ltd.: The Political Economy of Dependency, pp. 232-249. Edited by Robert Laxer. Toronto: McClelland and Stewart, 1973.

Laxer, James, and Laxer, Robert
The Liberal Idea of Canada. Toronto: James Lorimer, 1977.

Lemieux, Vincent, and Hudon, Raymond
Patronage et politique au Québec, 1944-1972. Sillery, Québec: Les Editions du Boréal Express, 1975.

Lévesque, René
An Option for Quebec. Toronto: McClelland and Stewart, 1968.

"René Lévesque for an Independent Quebec." Foreign Affairs 54 (July 1976).

Levitt, Joseph
Henri Bourassa and the Golden Calf: The Social Programme of the Nationalists of Quebec (1900-1914). Cahiers d'histoire, 3. Ottawa: Editions de l'Université d'Ottawa, 1969.

Levitt, Kari
"Towards Decolonization: Canada and Quebec." Canadian Forum 51 (March 1972).

Martell, George, ed.
"Our Schools Serve the Ruling Class: A CEQ White Paper." The Politics of the Canadian Public School, pp. 172-185. Edited by G. Martell. Toronto: James Lorimer, 1974.

QUEBEC (cont'd)

McRoberts, Kenneth, and Posgate, Dale
Quebec: Social Change and Political Crisis. Canada in Transition. Toronto: McClelland and Stewart, 1976.

Milner, Henry
"The Decline and Fall of the Quebec Liberal Regime: Contradictions in the Modern Quebec State." The Canadian State: Political Economy and Political Power, pp. 101-132. Edited by Leo Panitch. Toronto: University of Toronto Press, 1977.

Politics in the New Quebec. Toronto: McClelland and Stewart, 1978.

Milner, Sheilagh Hodgins, and Milner, Henry
The Decolonization of Quebec. A Carleton Contemporary. Toronto: McClelland and Stewart, 1973.

Monière, Denis
Le développement des idéologies au Québec: des origines à nos jours. Montréal: Editions Québec/Amérique, 1977.

Morin, Claude
Quebec vs. Ottawa: The Struggle for Self-Government, 1960-72. Toronto: University of Toronto Press, 1976.

Morris, Raymond N., and Lanphier, C. Michael
Three Scales of Inequality: Perspectives on French-English Relations. Canadian Social Problems. Toronto: Longmans, 1977.

Niosi, Jorge
"La nouvelle bourgeoisie canadien-française." Les Cahiers du Socialisme 1 (1978):5-50.

Ouellet, Fernand
Histoire économique et sociale du Québec, 1760-1850: structures et conjoncture. Montréal: Fides, 1966.

Parti Québécois
Qui controle l'économie du Québec? Le Citoyen, 3. Montréal: Editions du Parti Québécois, 1969.

Prochaine étape...quand nous serons vraiment chez nous. Montréal: Editions du Parti Québécois, 1972.

Pelletier, Gérard
The October Crisis. Toronto: McClelland and Stewart, 1971.

Pinard, Maurice
"Working Class Politics: An Interpretation of the Quebec Case." Canadian Review of Sociology and Anthropology 7:2 (1970):87-109.

QUEBEC (cont'd)

Pinard, Maurice
"Poverty and Political Movements in Quebec." Sociology Canada, pp. 308-320. Edited by C. Beattie and S. Crysdale. Toronto: Butterworth, 1974. Original in Social Problems 15:2 (Fall 1967): 250-263.

Piotte, Jean-Marc
"A Question of Strategy." Canadian Dimension 10:7 (March 1975).

Piotte, Jean-Marc; Ethier, D.; and Reynolds, J.
Les travailleurs contre l'état bourgeois. Montréal: L'Aurore, 1975.

Porter, John
"Canada: Dilemmas and Contradictions of a Multi-Ethnic Society." Sociology Canada, pp. 3-15. Edited by C. Beattie and S. Crysdale. Toronto: Butterworth, 1974.

Québec. Le ministre d'Etat au Développement culturel
La politique québécoise du développement culturel. 2 vol. Québec: Editeur officiel, 1978.

Raynauld, A.
Croissance et structures économiques de la province du Québec. Québec: Ministère de l'Industrie et du Commerce, 1961.

Le Propriété des entreprises au Québec: les années 60. Montréal: Les Presses de l'Université de Montréal, 1974.

Reid, M.
The Shouting Signpainters: A Literary and Political Account of Quebec Revolutionary Nationalism. Toronto: McClelland and Stewart, 1968.

Rempel, Henry David
"The Practice and Theory of the Fragile State: Trudeau's Conception of Authority." Journal of Canadian Studies 10:4 (November 1975):24-39.

Rioux, Marcel
Quebec in Question. 2nd ed. Toronto: James Lorimer, 1978. (Original 1969).

Rioux, Marcel, and Martin, Yves, eds.
French-Canadian Society. Vol. I. The Carleton Library, no. 18. Toronto: McClelland and Stewart, 1964.

Rotstein, A., ed.
Power Corrupted: The October Crisis and the Repression of Quebec. Toronto: New Press, 1971.

QUEBEC (cont'd)

Roussopoulos, D.
"Social Classes and Nationalism in Quebec." Our Generation 8:2 (Winter-April 1972):37-57.

Ryan, W.F.
The Clergy and Economic Growth in Quebec (1896-1914). Quebec: Les Presses de l'Université Laval, 1966.

Ryerson, Stanley B.
French Canada. Toronto: Progress Books, 1953.

Unequal Union. Toronto: Progress Books, 1968.

"Quebec: Concepts of Class and Nation." Capitalism and the National Question in Canada, pp. 211-227. Edited by G. Teeple. Toronto: University of Toronto Press, 1972.

Saint-Germain, M.
Une économie à libérer: le Québec analysé dans ses structures économiques. Montréal: Les Presses de l'Université de Montréal.

Saywell, John
The Rise of the Parti Quebecois. Toronto: University of Toronto Press, 1977.

Scott, Frank, and Oliver, Michael, eds.
Quebec States Her Case: Speeches and Articles from Quebec in the Years of Unrest. Toronto: Macmillan, 1964.

Siegried, André
The Race Question in Canada. The Carleton Library, no. 29. Edited by F.H. Underhill. Toronto: McClelland and Stewart, 1966.

Smith, Denis
Bleeding Hearts...Bleeding Country. Edmonton: Hurtig, 1971.

Stoddart, Jennifer
"The Woman Suffrage Bill in Quebec: Public Opinion as Reflected in the Press." Women in Canada, pp. 90-106. Edited by Marylee Stephenson. Toronto: New Press, 1973.

Surette, Ralph
"The Year of Manifestoes." Last Post 2:6 (July 1972):28-31.

Surette, Ralph; Davis, Bob; and Zannis, Mark
"The International Wolf Pack Moves in On the North." Last Post 3:3 (May 1973):24-30.

Taylor, Norman W.
"French Canadians as Industrial Entrepreneurs." Journal of Political Economy 68 (February 1969).

QUEBEC (cont'd)

Thompson, Dale, ed.
Quebec Society and Politics: Views from the Inside. Toronto: McClelland and Stewart, 1973.

Tremblay, Louis-Marie
Le syndicalisme québécois: idéologies de la C.S.N. et de la F.T.Q., 1940-1970. Montréal: Les Presses de l'Université de Montréal, 1970.

Tremblay, R.
Indépendance et marché common Québec--Etats-Unis; manifeste économique. Montréal: Editions du Jour, 1970.

Trudeau, Pierre Elliott
Federalism and the French Canadians. Toronto: Macmillan, 1968.

Trudeau, Pierre Elliott, ed.
The Asbestos Strike. Toronto: James, Lewis and Samuel, 1974. (First published 1956).

Vallières, Pierre
White Niggers of America. Toronto: McClelland and Stewart, 1971.

Choose. Toronto: New Press, 1972.

The Assassination of Pierre Laporte. Toronto: James Lorimer, 1977.

Wade, Mason
The French-Canadian Outlook: A Brief Account of the Unknown North Americans. The Carleton Library, no. 14. Toronto: McClelland and Stewart, 1964.

The French Canadians, 1760-1967. Rev. ed. 2 vols. Toronto: Macmillan, 1968.

IX. 'THE STAPLES': THIRTY BASIC READINGS IN CANADIAN POLITICAL ECONOMY

Berger, Thomas
Northern Frontier, Northern Homeland: The Report of the Mackenzie Valley Pipeline Inquiry. Ottawa: Supply and Services Canada, 1977.

Bourgault, Pierre
Innovation and the Structure of Canadian Industry. Ottawa: Science Council of Canada, 1972.

Canada. Department of National Revenue
Foreign Direct Investment in Canada. (The Gray Report). Ottawa: Information Canada, 1972.

Clement, Wallace
Continental Corporate Power: Economic Elite Linkages Between Canada and the United States. Toronto: McClelland and Stewart, 1977.

Crean, Susan M.
Who's Afraid of Canadian Culture? Don Mills, Ont.: General Publishing, 1976.

Creighton, Donald G.
The Empire of the St. Lawrence. Toronto: Macmillan, 1956.

Easterbrook, W.T., and Watkins, Mel, eds.
Approaches to Canadian Economic History: A Selection of Essays. Toronto: McClelland and Stewart, 1967.

Godfrey, David, and Watkins, Mel, eds.
Gordon to Watkins to You: A Documentary; The Battle for Control of Our Economy. Toronto: New Press, 1970.

Grant, George
Lament for a Nation: The Defeat of Canadian Nationalism. Toronto: McClelland and Stewart, 1965.

Hardin, Herschel
A Nation Unaware: The Canadian Economic Culture. Vancouver: J.J. Douglas Ltd., 1974.

Innis, Harold A.
The Fur Trade in Canada: An Introduction to Canadian Economic History. Rev. ed. Toronto: University of Toronto Press, 1956. (First published 1930).

Essays in Canadian Economic History. Edited by Mary Q. Innis. Toronto: University of Toronto Press, 1957.

'THE STAPLES': THIRTY BASIC READINGS IN CANADIAN POLITICAL ECONOMY (cont'd)

Kierans, Eric
Report on Natural Resources Policy in Manitoba. Winnipeg: Queen's Printer, 1973.

Laxer, James, and Laxer, Robert
The Liberal Idea of Canada: Pierre Trudeau and the Question of Canada's Survival. Toronto: James Lorimer, 1977.

Levitt, Kari
Silent Surrender: The Multinational Corporation in Canada. Toronto: Macmillan, 1970.

Lipton, Charles
The Trade Union Movement of Canada, 1827-1959. Toronto: NC Press, 1973.

Lumsden, Ian, ed.
Close the 49th Parallel, Etc.: The Americanization of Canada. Toronto: University of Toronto Press, 1970.

Marshall, Herbert; Southard, Frank; and Taylor, Kenneth W.
Canadian-American Industry: A Study in International Investment. The Carleton Library, no. 93. Toronto: McClelland and Stewart, 1976. (First published 1936).

Mathias, Philip
Forced Growth. Toronto: James Lorimer, 1971.

McRoberts, Kenneth, and Posgate, Dale
Quebec: Social Change and Political Crisis. Canada in Transition. Toronto: McClelland and Stewart, 1976.

Milner, Sheilagh Hodgins, and Milner, Henry
The Decolonization of Quebec: An Analysis of Left-Wing Nationalism. A Carleton Contemporary. Toronto: McClelland and Stewart, 1973.

Naylor, R.T.
The History of Canadian Business, 1867-1914. 2 vols. Toronto: James Lorimer, 1975.

Panitch, Leo, ed.
The Canadian State: Political Economy and Political Power. Toronto: University of Toronto Press, 1977.

Park, Frank, and Park, Libbie
Anatomy of Big Business. Toronto: James, Lewis and Samuel, 1973.

Pratt, Larry
The Tar Sands: Syncrude and the Politics of Oil. Edmonton: Hurtig, 1976.

'THE STAPLES': THIRTY BASIC READINGS IN CANADIAN POLITICAL ECONOMY (cont'd)

Ryerson, Stanley
Unequal Union: Confederation and the Roots of Conflict in the Canadas, 1815-1873. Toronto: Progress Books, 1968.

The Founding of Canada. 2nd ed. Toronto: Progress Books, 1975. (First published 1960).

Stephenson, Marylee, ed.
Women in Canada. 2nd ed. Don Mills, Ont.: General Publishing, 1977. (First published 1973).

Teeple, Gary, ed.
Capitalism and the National Question in Canada. Toronto: University of Toronto Press, 1972.

Vallières, Pierre
White Niggers of America. Toronto: McClelland and Stewart, 1971.

FURTHER SOURCES

For those interested in the research and study of the Canadian political economy, subscribe to the Canadian Political Economy Newsletter. It appears at least twice during the academic year and contains information on conferences, research activity, bibliographic and other information for people working in this field.

Write to Daniel Drache
c/o Dept. of Political Science
York University
4700 Keele St.
Downsview, Ont.

Cost: $3.50 per year.

The following Canadian periodicals frequently have articles relevant to Political Economy and serve as a continuing up-date:

<u>Alternatives</u>
<u>Canadian Dimension</u>
<u>The Canadian Forum</u>
<u>City Magazine</u>
<u>Journal of Canadian Studies</u>
<u>Labour/le Travailleur</u>
<u>Last Post</u>
<u>LAWG Letter</u>
<u>Next Year Country</u>
<u>Ontario Report</u>
<u>Our Generation</u>
<u>This Magazine</u>

Canada's Visual History, Series 1

For Ontario, Quebec, and the four Atlantic Provinces, purchase orders should be directed to the exclusive NFB distributor:

Visual Education Centre
115 Berkeley Street
Toronto, Ontario M5A 2W8
Phone: (416) 363-4436

For the four western provinces, the Northwest Territories, and the Yukon, purchase orders should be directed to the exclusive NFB distributor:

Harry Smith & Sons Ltd.
1150 Homer Street
Vancouver, B.C. V6B 2X8

For information on current research and recent reports on a very wide range of study on women, consult the *Canadian Newsletter of Research on Women*. It comes out three times a year and each issue is over 100 pages in length. Virtually all university libraries carry it or it can be ordered: c/o Department of Sociology, O.I.S.E., 252 Bloor Street West, Toronto, Ontario. ($7.00 for individual subscriptions, $15.00 for institutions)

INDEX